Blessed

Is the

Daughter

*God make you like Sarah, Rebecca,
Rachel, and Leah.*

Parents thus bless their daughters on the eve of the Sabbath and festivals.

*No generation can be redeemed
except through the merit of the
righteous women of that era.*
　　　　　　　　　—Midrash

Blessed

Is the

Daughter

Edited by Carolyn Starman Hessel

SHENGOLD BOOKS

Rockville, Maryland   New York

Published by:

SHENGOLD BOOKS
An imprint of Schreiber Publishing, Inc.
Post Office Box 4193
Rockville, MD 20849 USA
www.schreibernet.com
spbooks@aol.com

Library of Congress Cataloging-in-Publication Data

Blessed is the daughter / edited by Carolyn Starman Hessel.
    p.   cm.
    Includes bibliographical references and index.
    Summary: Relates the stories of heroic Jewish women who helped their people and all people, from Biblical times to today.
    ISBN 1-887563-44-X (alk. paper)
    1. Jewish women Biography Juvenile literature. 2. Women in Judaism Juvenile literature.   [1. Jews Biography. 2. Women Biography. 3. Women in Judaism.]   I. Hessel, Carolyn Starman.
DS115.2.B55   1999
920.72'089'924--dc21
[B]   99-10068
                                        CIP

Contents

Acknowledgments

This book represents the composite effort of many people. It began with the work of the original editors, Meyer Waxman, Shulamith Ish-Kishor, and Jacob Sloan, and the publisher of the original version, Moshe Sheinbaum, whose work has made this an inspirational book for many readers since 1959, in both word and image.

The present remake of the book (actually the eighth edition, if we count the first seven) is the result of the dedicated efforts of writers, editors, and graphic designers to whom this has been a labor of love. This work was initiated under the guidance of Carolyn Starman Hessel, executive director of the Jewish Book Council.

Special thanks to our new contributors: Rachel Schreiber, assistant professor of photography and women's studies at the Herron School of Art in Indianapolis; Michal Friedlander, Blumenthal Curator of Judaica at the Judah L. Magnes Museum in Berkeley; and Rabbi Tobie Weisman.

A word of thanks to our page layout and text editor, Julie Plovnick, for her conscientious work, to Mark Sabatke for the graphic work, and to Debra Valencia for the book jacket.

Many institutions, organizations, and individuals contributed photographs and art work for this volume. They are acknowledged next to each item. But a special word of thanks is due to the *Washington Jewish Week*, the Embassy of Israel in Washington, D.C., the Jewish Museum in New York, the Judah L. Magnes Museum in Berkeley, artists Judy Chicago and Deborah Kass, and Mary Boone Gallery.

The publisher takes special joy in the fact that *Blessed Is the Daughter*, originally a pioneer in the field of literature on great women, can be offered once again to the public, with updated information on what women have achieved in recent years.

—*Mordecai Schreiber*

Introduction

Blessed Is the Daughter was first issued in 1959 in recognition of the importance of women and their inherent equality in Judaism. Thus, it foreshadowed the events of the 1960s and '70s which have radically changed the status of women. For nearly four decades it has been a popular book in the English-speaking Jewish world, appearing in a new edition every three years. Over time, the cultural and religious role of women in society at large and in Judaism in particular has reached far beyond anything imaginable forty years ago. For this reason, the book had to be practically rewritten.

Not only has the book been updated through the end of the twentieth century, the editors and authors have gone back in time and reexamined the key stories about Jewish women in the Bible, the Talmud, and during the Islamic and Christian periods up to modern times. This act of revision showed clearly that the role of women in Judaism has not always been fully recognized and appreciated. Yet, despite this oversight or even deliberate bias, history has left us a record of remarkable Jewish women throughout the ages. This book identifies some fifty such women, beginning with our mother Sarah in the Book of Genesis, and leading up to some of today's best-known women, who have made a great difference in the history of their people in nearly every field.

These fifty women are by no means the only ones who have made a difference. They represent hundreds and thousands of other women of their time and of all time, without whom the Jewish people would not be here today. Consider the case of Miriam, Moses' older sister, who saved him as an infant by turning him over to Pharaoh's daughter. Or Rachel, the wife of Rabbi Akiva, without whom this great codifier of the written and oral Law would never have been able to do the work he did. During the dark days of the Spanish Inquisition and later under tyrannical rulers in Europe, women like Doña Gracia Nasi and Glueckel of Hameln showed how the spirit of Judaism was stronger than any tyrant, secular or religious, who sought to break it. In nineteenth-century America, Rebecca Gratz laid the groundwork for social work and for Jewish religious education, while Emma Lazarus saw the nation as the "mother of exiles" and dreamed in her poetry of the Jews' return to their ancestral land.

Equally remarkable is the role of Jewish women in American society and in the Jewish world in the early twentieth century. Here we find social reformers like Lillian Wald and Emma Goldman; organizers like Henrietta Szold, the founder of Hadassah and one of the early Zionist leaders; and great performers of the Yiddish and American stage like Molly Picon. In the middle of the century we find heroic women like Zivia Lubetkin and Hannah Szenes, who experienced the long night of the Holocaust, and we realize what a vast contribution women made to the establishment of the State of Israel. But it was not until the last third of the century that Jewish women began to distinguish themselves in practically every area of human endeavor. These years saw the first Jewish women in space and in the U.S. Congress, Senate, and Supreme Court, as well as the first Jewish woman prime minister of Israel. For the first time, Jewish women became rabbis and were Nobel prize winners in literature and science. And the list goes on.

As the twenty-first century unfolds, one cannot help but feel that women have only just begun to show the world how much they can accomplish. Had women been given more equality in the past, their contributions would have been even greater than what is conveyed in this book. In the future, when women at long last have achieved full equality, there will be no difference between what men and women can do and accomplish. In a world where a person is judged strictly on merit, regardless of gender, race, religion, nationality, or any other form of differentiation, each person will achieve his or her full potential. Women no doubt will play a critical role in bringing about such a world.

In reading about the women in this book we learn that the true measure of their greatness is not their intellectual, political, artistic, or financial achievement. It is rather the quality of their character, their care for others, their sense of justice, and the fact that all are proud daughters of their people, as can be seen not so much in their words as in their actions.

In an age when many people have grown cynical about leaders and leadership, when it is difficult to find good role models, it helps to remind ourselves that there have been, and there still are today, great women we can admire, and who can still inspire us to strive for excellence and work for a better world. One is reminded of the words of Golda Meir in her memoirs, when she talks about people like Zivia Lubetkin and the other fighters of the Warsaw Ghetto, who in their fearless yet hopeless struggle against the Nazi beast inspired the fighters for Israel's independence to stand few against many and prevail, and later the words of Lubetkin herself, who, having survived the Holocaust, tells us that people like Golda Meir and the other pioneers in the Land of Israel inspired her and her friends in the Warsaw Ghetto to undertake such a hopeless struggle not because they expected to win, but because they knew that the Warsaw Ghetto was not the end of the Jewish people, but only a prelude to the rebirth of this people in its ancient land.

Not all of us can be movers and shakers. Nor are we expected to be. But we all have the opportunity to strive to do better, to reach out and help others, and to uphold the values enunciated by the prophets of Israel so long ago, "It was told to you, children of man and woman, what is good, and what the Almighty demands of you, only to do justice, and to love mercy, and to walk humbly with the Almighty, your God."

Chapter One

Blessed Is the Daughter

You are now taking your first steps as a young woman. The world is changing before your very eyes. People are beginning to expect of you a certain amount of responsibility. Your opinion is becoming more important; your family is beginning to be concerned about what you are going to be rather than what you are at this moment. You are seeking new friendships, new groups where you fit in. And you are beginning to dream, as all young women do, about your chances for happiness in the decisions you will make as an adult.

While these thoughts, these changes, these hopes and fears and wondering are common to all young women at all times and in all places, you are surely aware that for you, as a Jew, there will be a few more challenges. But do you know that there are also very great rewards?

You are a daughter of a people few in number but supremely gifted, a nation with an old and great culture on this earth, a nation whose people wrote one of the noblest books ever written, at a time when their physical life was at its most primitive, that is, while they plowed the soil with sticks, lived in tents, took pitchers to the well to draw water, and counted their wealth in heads of cattle. From this Bible of the Hebrews came the Law which has guided the Western world from that day on.

Many daughters have done valiantly, but you have surpassed them all.
—Proverbs 31:29

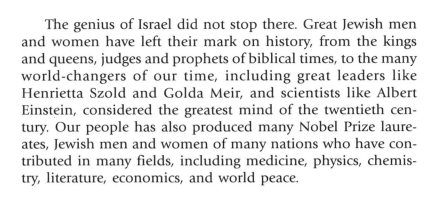

The genius of Israel did not stop there. Great Jewish men and women have left their mark on history, from the kings and queens, judges and prophets of biblical times, to the many world-changers of our time, including great leaders like Henrietta Szold and Golda Meir, and scientists like Albert Einstein, considered the greatest mind of the twentieth century. Our people has also produced many Nobel Prize laureates, Jewish men and women of many nations who have contributed in many fields, including medicine, physics, chemistry, literature, economics, and world peace.

We Jews have always felt close to our God. We have fiercely resisted all efforts to deprive us of the spiritual power which has helped us through terrible trials, not without losses but with the final victory in our hands.

As a Jewish woman, you are blessed with the opportunity to become one more golden link in the four thousand-year-old chain of Jewish life. While reading or browsing through this book, you will discover that women have always played a crucial role in the life of our people, from the time of our mother Sarah, the first Jewish woman, to today. This role has not been restricted to the home, although the home was where the Jewish woman provided the foundation upon which Jewish life endured and flourished even in times of great poverty and persecution. While the outside world was often harsh and cold, the Jewish home was warm and safe, mainly because of the role women played as wives, mothers, homemakers, often co-providers, and usually the ones who saw things through practical and wise eyes, helping their families put everything in perspective, assuaging pain in times of trouble, and bringing joy to all happy occasions.

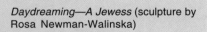

Daydreaming—A Jewess (sculpture by Rosa Newman-Walinska)

But perhaps there is a question in your mind. Perhaps you are thinking that because Judaism was born in the ancient Near East, most Jews still believe that women are the inferior sex, and that you, in embracing the Jewish community, would be forced to compromise your individuality and status. As you will see in reading the sections in this book about women in biblical and Talmudic times, while the Jews in ancient times did live surrounded by nations who relegated women to a position of inferiority, in the Jewish community women were far from inferior. A single early biblical example clearly illustrates this point. In the period of the Judges, before the Hebrew tribes became united into one nation, the most towering figure was a woman named Deborah, who judged her people and led the tribes of Israel to victory against their Canaanite enemies.

Still, you might say, isn't it true that the Hebrews in biblical times practiced polygamy, whereby one man was allowed to have more than one wife at the same time?

Polygamy was practiced in ancient times because life was a bitter struggle against nature and required large families to cope with it. Family groups or tribes consisting of one man and two or more wives ensured the group's survival. But unlike the surrounding cultures, the Hebrews never formed harems, where women were confined as in a prison, with no object in life but to please the man who owned them. Even though King Solomon had many wives, most were princesses of foreign nations whom he married to establish peace with those nations. Polygamy, as you will see elsewhere in this book, became less common even in biblical times, was rarely practiced thereafter, and was officially abolished among Jews in medieval Europe.

You may also have heard that a Hebrew girl was not allowed to choose her husband, that her marriage was arranged for her, even against her will. Well, let us consider the case of our mother Sarah's son, Isaac, and his bride, Rebecca. Abraham wanted his son, Isaac, to marry the right woman, so he sent his servant Eliezer on a long journey to the city of Nahor. There Eliezer thought not of the beauty of the hoped-for bride, but of her kindness and intelligence. When he asked Rebecca's family to let her marry Isaac, they replied, "We will call Rebecca and ask her." And they asked Rebecca, "Will you go with this man (to marry Isaac)?" And she said, "I will go."

The Fifth Commandment says, "You shall honor your father and your mother." No difference is made between parents. The Book of Proverbs urges, "Obey the commandment of your father, and forget not the teaching of your mother." In this book, husbands are emphatically warned against turning away from "the wife of your youth" and are told to avoid "the other woman, for her path is the way of death." In the Hebrew language, the words for "wisdom" and "industriousness" are feminine. The Book of Proverbs concludes with a song of praise to the Jewish woman, not merely for her beauty and charm but also for her strength, her business acumen, her intelligence, her tact, and her skill in organizing and running the household.

I am the Lord your God.
You shall not have any other gods.
You shall not take the name of the Lord your God in vain.
Remember the Sabbath day and keep it holy.
Honor your father and your mother.
You shall not murder.
You shall not commit adultery.
You shall not steal.
You shall not commit perjury.
You shall not covet.

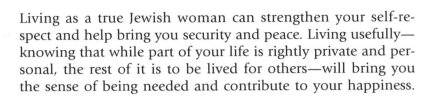

Living as a true Jewish woman can strengthen your self-respect and help bring you security and peace. Living usefully—knowing that while part of your life is rightly private and personal, the rest of it is to be lived for others—will bring you the sense of being needed and contribute to your happiness.

For the Jewish woman especially, her usefulness must extend beyond herself and her own family. For years, Jewish women's organizations in the U.S., in Israel, and throughout the world have made enormous contributions to the welfare of Jews everywhere and to society as a whole. Elsewhere in this book we will discuss some of those organizations and some of the outstanding Jewish women who have left their mark on their people and on the world.

Israeli paratrooper

Not all of us can or need be nation-savers or world-shakers, but we can all gain from helping others. We may not know any heroic women personally, but we all know and appreciate women—of whom there are many among the Jews—who give kindness, hospitality, sympathy, and warmth to all who come. To be such a woman is to be a true daughter of Israel.

Emma Lazarus, a famous American Jewish poet of the nineteenth century, wrote the following words in a poem now inscribed on the Statue of Liberty in New York:

Give me your tired, your poor,
Your huddled masses yearning to breathe free.

The words "yearning to breathe free" could serve as the motto for all Jewish women today. More than ever before in history, Jewish women in the United States, in Israel, and throughout the world are working towards full equality and freedom in all areas of human endeavor, from culture and religion to everyday activities. During the last quarter of the twentieth century, Jewish women, especially in the United States, have assumed roles once unheard of, such as the first astronaut, and the first Supreme Court Justice. Also during that time women began to serve as rabbis, and as the number of women rabbis continues to grow, women are exerting an ever greater influence on the Jewish religion.

Bella Abzug, a women's rights activist and the first Jewish woman to serve in the U.S. Congress, once said, "Women have been trained to speak softly and carry a lipstick. Those days are over."

This is a very exciting time to be a young Jewish woman. In word and image, this book seeks to capture the struggles and achievements of Jewish women, past and present. It seeks to instruct and inspire, to prove that despite inequality, women have played a decisive role in guiding our people's destiny for some four thousand years, as far back as our mother Sarah. You will see that without their love and wisdom, our people would not be where they are today. But most important, you will discover that the accomplishments of great Jewish women have paved the way for you as you plan your future.

Camp Massad, Pennsylvania

Hannah Szenes, a young kibbutz poet who died fighting the Nazis, wrote:

Blessed is the match that burned and kindled flames,
Blessed is the flame that set hearts on fire.

Not all of us are called upon to offer the supreme sacrifice. But as members of a people that transformed the world, young Jewish women seek greater freedom and equality not only for self gain but for a higher purpose, defined by the Jewish prayer book as *tikkun olam b'malchut shaddai,* or "perfecting the world in the image of the divine." This they have already begun to do. Let us hope that coming generations of young Jewish women will continue in this spirit. In the words of the book of Proverbs in the Hebrew Bible:

Many daughters have done valiantly,
But you have surpassed them all.

This picture, taken in present-day Israel, reminds us of biblical times.

Qumran Caves, near the Dead Sea, yielded in 1948 the Dead Sea Scrolls,
one of the greatest archeological discoveries of the twentieth century.

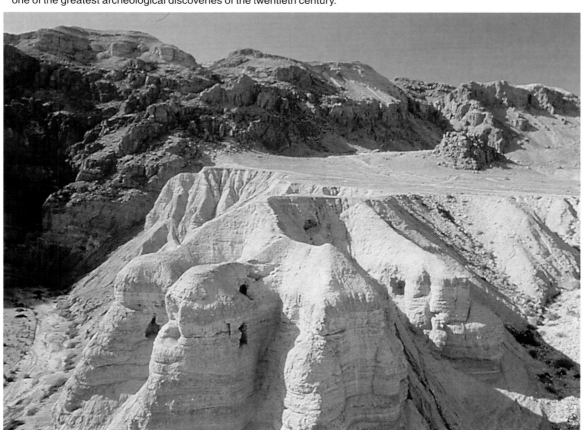

A view of northern Israel

Military parade along the walls of the Old City of Jerusalem

Chapter Two

Jewish Women in Biblical Times

In Judaism, men and women are created equal. The Bible states this fundamental belief very clearly, telling the story of God's creation of all life: "Male and female were they created." The same act of creation produced both man and woman, making them equal from the very beginning. Both were created in the image of God. Although God first created man and then took a rib from Adam's side to create Eve, both were created in the same spirit, in the same image.

Woman's equality with man is stressed in yet another verse describing the creation of human beings: "On the day God created man, in the likeness of God was man created; male and female were they created, and they were blessed, and their name was called Adam, on the day they were created."

The Zohar, the holy book of Jewish mysticism, explains why the Bible uses the plural in referring to Adam: "The Bible says, 'God blessed them and called their name Adam,' not 'God blessed him and called his name Adam.' This is intended to show us that God's blessing and the name of Adam belong to both man and woman, equally."

Indeed, our sages in the Midrash took this verse to mean that at first God created only one human being who was neither male nor female. Only when God noticed that the new being was lonely was the decision made to create a human pair—male and female, who would complement and help each other.

Is God in Judaism male or female? Throughout time, both Jews and non-Jews have pictured God as masculine. Many non-Jews even believe that God once assumed a human form—

Sculpture in wood by
Chaim Gross

17

Sarah on a recent stamp
(painting by Abel Pann)

God make you like Sarah,
Rebecca, Rachel, and Leah.
—Parents thus bless their
daughters on the eve of
the Sabbath and festivals.

that of a male. In the Hebrew Bible, however, God is neither male nor female. While it is true that the Bible uses the second and third person masculine forms of "you" and "he" in referring to God, we must bear in mind that the Hebrew language does not have a separate word for "it," and that masculine forms like "he" are also used in Hebrew in the sense of "it."

Great Jewish scholars like Maimonides have taught us that God has no human form and no gender. When the Bible, for example, refers to God in some places as a "man of war," this term is used only as a metaphor to illustrate God's mighty acts, which resemble those of a warrior. When Moses asks God to reveal Himself, God replies, "I am what I am," refusing to offer any physical description. In the Jewish tradition, attributing a gender to God is misunderstanding the nature of God.

Maimonides goes on to say that the reason the Bible uses human forms and attributes to describe God is to make God easier to understand, yet none of these descriptions are to be taken literally. Indeed, among the many descriptions of God in the Bible are both masculine and feminine forms. For example, the presence of God, called *shkhinah* in Hebrew, is a feminine term. In short, God is neither male nor female. Instead, all the aspects and attributes of both genders are combined within the concept of God, making God equally accessible to both men and women.

The Hebrew Bible tells the story of great men and women and their relationship to God, beginning with the founders of the Jewish people, our father Abraham and our mother Sarah. Jews believe that God has protected them and enabled them to last all these centuries because of the merit of their three fathers, or patriarchs—Abraham, Isaac, and Jacob—and their four mothers, or matriarchs—Sarah, Rebecca, Leah, and Rachel.

Sarah is the one who helped Abraham endure his many trials and tribulations and give rise to a new nation.

Rebecca is the one who, when her husband Isaac became blind and could not distinguish between his sons Jacob and Esau, made sure that Jacob would receive his father's blessing and become the founder of the twelve tribes of Israel.

Leah is the one who gave birth to Judah and to five other sons of Jacob, thereby fulfilling God's promise to Abraham: "I will make you into a great nation."

Rachel is the one who gave birth to Joseph, who in turn would save his brothers from famine. She remains to this day the symbolic mother of Israel who prays for her children to return from exile.

The Talmud and the Midrash contain many legends about our mother Sarah. According to one legend, Sarah was so beautiful that when the casket where Abraham hid her when they came to Egypt was forced open, her beauty flooded all of Egypt with light. When the Pharaoh, king of Egypt, saw Sarah, he immediately fell in love with her and wrote her a marriage contract on the spot, bequeathing her all his possessions. He relented only when he learned that Abraham was her husband. He gave Sarah the province of Goshen, which her descendants later occupied as their rightful possession. But most remarkable of all, Pharaoh gave Sarah his daughter Hagar to be her handmaid. He preferred that Hagar serve Sarah rather than another woman.

And God appeared to him at the terebinth trees of Mamreh . . . And behold, three men stood before him . . . and they asked, "Where is Sarah, your wife?"
—Genesis 18

Sarah and Abraham's terebinth tree in Hebron (Germany, 1896)

According to the Bible, Sarah's only son, Isaac, was destined to give rise to a great nation, through which all other nations of the earth would be blessed. When Sarah became aware of the threat to her son posed by his half-brother Ishmael, Hagar's son, she sent away Hagar and Ishmael. Some may argue that Sarah was being cruel and unfair. But in reality she was doing only what God had ordered her to do.

Equally controversial is Rebecca's act of deceiving her old, blind husband, Isaac, to secure his blessing for Jacob while taking it away from Jacob's twin brother, Esau. In his old age Isaac loved to·feast on game that his son Esau, the hunter, used to bring back from the field. When Rebecca learned that Isaac had ordered Esau to bring him choice meat for a feast so that he, Isaac, could bless Esau and make him heir, she arranged for her other son, Jacob, to pose as Esau before his blind father and bring him a homemade feast, thus securing his blessing.

Jewish legend insists that Rebecca's act was justified, for she was motivated not by favoritism toward Jacob, but rather by a deep conviction that Esau was not destined by God to receive Isaac's blessing. So, when Jacob hesitated to follow Rebecca's bidding and win his father's blessing through deceit, his mother said to him, according to legend: "Do as I say, for you are my son whose children, every one of them, will be righteous and God-fearing. Not one will be lacking in faith." It was for the sake of Jacob's children, who gave rise to the tribes of Israel, that Rebecca had to do what she did.

The Meeting of Rebecca and Eliezer at the Well (etching by Teyssonnières, after Tiepolo)

Rachel, the third of the great matriarchs, is also credited as having shown remarkable virtue. She is said to have warned Jacob of her father Laban's intention to substitute her sister, Leah, for herself on the wedding night. Rachel and Jacob agreed on a sign by which Jacob might recognize his true love. But when Rachel saw Leah being led into the marriage hall, she stifled her great love for Jacob, so as not to put her sister to shame, and told Leah the agreed upon sign.

According to the Bible, Rachel was buried on the road to Ephrat, outside Jerusalem. Legend has it that Jacob selected this site. Gifted with the power of prophecy, Jacob knew that the Hebrews would pass this point on their march to exile in Babylonia. As the exiles passed by Rachel's grave, she would ask God to show her children mercy. That is why the prophet Jeremiah, in one of his consoling prophecies, sees Rachel in a vision rising from her grave:

> *A voice was heard in Ramah, lamentation and bitter weeping;*
> *Rachel weeping for her children, refusing to be comforted.*
> *Thus says the Lord: Refrain from weeping, and wipe your tears,*

*For your work will be rewarded, your children shall
return from captivity.*

❦   ❦   ❦

After the time of the ancestors, the next great female personality in the Bible is Miriam. Born in Egypt during the time of
Hebrew slavery, she was destined to play an important role
alongside her younger brother, Moses, in liberating her people
from Egyptian bondage and
leading them through the
desert to the Promised Land.
Miriam watched over Moses
from the time of his birth.
When Moses was born, his
mother was expected to follow Pharaoh's command and
drown her newborn son in
the Nile River. Instead, she put
him in a basket and hid him
among the bulrushes growing
alongside the river. Miriam hid
nearby and watched as
Pharaoh's daughter and her
servants approached the river
to bathe. She arranged for the
princess to take the baby, thus
saving his life.

Miriam the Prophet (nineteenth-
century engraving)

When Moses took his people out of Egypt and split the
Red Sea so that they could cross it on dry land, Miriam led the
women of Israel in song and dance, saying:

> *Sing to the Lord for these mighty deeds,
> Horse and rider were cast into the sea.*

Miriam was given the title of prophet (Exodus 15:20), the
same title given to her brother, Moses (Deuteronomy 34:10).
Here again the Bible makes it clear that women can attain the
same rank as men, no matter how lofty. Indeed, Jewish tradition records that the day Miriam died, the well of water which
accompanied the Israelites during their trek from Egypt to the
Promised Land disappeared. From this our sages learned that
because of Miriam's merit the people of Israel did not perish
in the desert from thirst.

The Talmud says: "Because of righteous women, Israel was
redeemed from Egypt." In the time of the exodus, as in the

time of the ancestors, women always played a critical role in securing the welfare and survival of the Jewish people.

❧   ❧   ❧

You may wonder, why does the Bible give men a great deal more coverage than women? Most likely, the Bible was narrated by men who told mostly about men. The same is true about world literature and history in general, from the ancient Greeks and Romans to our own time. Yet keep in mind that more than a few women—matriarchs, prophets, queens, and plain, ordinary women—figure prominently in the Bible. Two books in the Bible, the Scroll of Ruth and the Scroll of Esther, are named after women. The Bible as a whole is a book of few words and deep meaning. Like an iceberg, only a small part of its meaning and message can be seen above the surface, while the rest remains hidden. Thus, there are many brief references to women scattered throughout the Bible which, though easy to miss, speak volumes.

Song of Deborah, by Inbal dancers

Courtesy of the America-Israel Culture Foundation

The Book of Exodus offers an example: As the Israelites wandered through the desert, the five daughters of Zelophehad, from the tribe of Manasseh, approached Moses and the elders and told them that their father had died and left no sons, and that they wished to inherit his estate. This is probably one of the earliest cases on record of daughters claiming their right of inheritance. God told Moses and the elders to establish new inheritance laws, mandating that a father who has only daughters can pass his inheritance on to those daughters instead of to his brothers, as was the practice until then.

Soon after the Hebrew tribes entered the Promised Land and began to settle it, they were attacked by their neighbors. In the absence of a great leader of Moses' or Joshua's stature, a woman named Deborah the Prophet came forth and completed Joshua's conquest of the land. She ordered Barak, the chief of the tribes of Naphtali and Zebulun, to raise an army and liberate a large part of the land that was under the rule of Yabin, the most powerful of the Canaanite kings. Barak called on Deborah to accompany his forces and inspire his troops, saying the war would be lost without her presence. Deborah agreed; together with Barak she led the tribal army to victory, uniting the entire country under Jewish rule. In celebration of this triumph, Deborah, a poet as well as a judge and prophet, composed a song of victory. You can find it in the Bible, in the fifth chapter of Judges. One of the finest heroic poems in world literature, it includes these stirring verses:

> *Awake, awake, O Deborah, awake, awake and sing,*
> *Arise, Barak, arise and capture your enemies;*
> *You, the remnant of your people's mighty warriors.*
> *The Lord came down among the mighty . . .*
> *The stars in their orbits fought against Siserah . . .*
> *So may all your enemies perish, O Lord,*
> *And those who love you shine like the sun in all its*
> > *glory.*

As the tribes of Israel became more unified, they chose a king to rule over them. Here we come across a remarkable woman by the name of Ruth. The Bible dedicates an entire book to Ruth, one of the most beloved women in world literature. Ruth was a Moabite woman married to a Jewish man who died young. After his death his mother, Naomi, decided to return to her land. Not expecting her daughter-in-law to go with her, Naomi told Ruth to return to her parents' home. But Ruth refused, telling Naomi:

Ruth and Boaz (nineteenth-century engraving)

> *Do not ask me*
> *to leave you;*
> > *for wherever you*
> *go I will go,*
> *Wherever you stay I*
> *will stay; your people*
> *are my people,*
> > *Your God is my God.*
> > *Wherever you die I will die . . .*

Today, when a woman converts to Judaism, these words are read in the conversion ceremony, for Ruth is the best example of a woman who chose to become part of the Jewish people. Her reward was indeed great. She became the ances-

23

tor of David, Israel's most beloved king.

When it comes to romantic love in the Bible, nothing surpasses the book called Song of Songs. It is attributed to King Solomon, King David's son. In this book, which according to tradition was written when Solomon was a young man, the young king falls in love with a shepherd girl named Shulamit. He courts her with the following words:

> *You are lovely, my beloved, you are lovely,*
> *Your eyes are like doves.*

To which she responds:

> *You are lovely, my love, you are pleasant . . .*

She goes on to say:

> *Like an apple tree among the trees of the forest,*
> *So is my love among men;*
> *I choose to rest in his shadow, I desire his fruit.*
> *. . . comfort me with apples, for I am lovesick.*

Interestingly, throughout this book the young woman is given equal time to express her emotions, no less than the powerful king himself. She is not a meek and obedient servant of the king, but rather an equal whose words of love are no less beautiful and imaginative than those of the king. She does not refer to the king as her master or superior. Rather, he is her love, her companion, her beloved, and she is his mate, the one he loves. Our rabbis of blessed memory were so taken with this book that they proclaimed it to be a love story between God, represented by the king, and the Jewish people, represented by Shulamit the shepherd girl.

After the death of Solomon, his kingdom was split into two smaller kingdoms, Israel in the north and Judea in the south. The kingdom of Israel lasted for only about two hundred years before it was destroyed and ten of the twelve tribes of Israel were lost. The kingdom of Judea lasted for another two centuries but eventually was also overrun by powerful enemies and its people exiled. One country where Judea's exiles settled was Persia, which later became a mighty empire. In Persia lived a remarkable Jewish woman named Esther, for whom another book in the Bible is named. Because of her uncommon beauty and wisdom, Esther became the queen of the Persian Empire. God could not have chosen a better place

Scroll of Esther

24

and time for Esther to become queen. During her reign the Jews who lived in the empire came under mortal danger when the chief counselor to the king, the wicked Haman, plotted to kill them all. Esther learned about the plot through her cousin, Mordecai. Now we discover that in addition to her beauty and wisdom, Esther was also a woman of uncommon courage. She was not afraid to confront Haman in the presence of the king and expose his plot. Haman was executed, and the Jews were saved. Every year on Purim the Jews celebrate Esther and Mordecai's victory over Haman.

Haman pleads for his life before Esther (Edward Armitage, 1817-96).

The above examples clearly show that from Israel's early beginnings women did much more than stay home and let men make all the important decisions. We also saw that back in antiquity, when women were generally the property of their fathers and husbands, Israelite society accorded women far more rights and freedoms than were known in other societies in those days. To this day, the Hebrew Bible is one of humanity's main sources of laws which protect the rights of all people and preserve the dignity of every person, male and female alike.

Biblical women on stamps. Left to right: Hulda the Prophet; Ruth the Moabite; Hannah, mother of the prophet Samuel

Naomi and Her Daughters-in-law, by Gustave Doré. "For wherever you go I will go . . ." —Ruth 1:16

Chapter Three

Heroic Women in the Maccabean Period

The Maccabean period, which followed the biblical period, is best known for the heroic deeds of Judah Maccabee and his fearless brothers. When we celebrate Hanukkah, we sing the praises of the Maccabees, who, though few in number, won incredible victories against the mighty armies of Antiochus, the ruler of the Greco-Syrian Empire who sought to do away with Judaism. What we often forget is that this period also produced several heroic women who have been the subject of many legends not only in our tradition but also in world literature.

Judah Maccabee

The first of those heroic women was Hannah, the mother of the seven sons seized by King Antiochus when he began to persecute the Jews. When Hannah's sons were commanded to eat pork, they refused. Hannah supported their decision and gave them the courage to endure frightful torture. One by one they were executed in their mother's presence. When the time came for the youngest son to die, the king pleaded with Hannah to persuade the boy to eat pork and thus spare his life. She refused, and the youngest met the same fate as his older brothers. Hannah's subsequent death is reported in several different versions. The Midrash maintains that she died by jumping from a roof. Elsewhere we are told that she fell dead atop her children's corpses. In the Book of Maccabees we are told that she threw herself into the fire. Hannah's martyrdom became an example for Jews throughout the centuries who were willing to die for *kiddush ha'shem*, or the sanctification of God's name, rather than give up their heritage and beliefs.

Another heroic Jewish woman whose story was written around the same period is Judith. As in the case of Hannah, here too the story is shrouded in legend, and we have little proof that either woman really existed. Moreover, the story of Judith, unlike that of Hannah, is not set in the time of the Maccabees, but rather two (some say four) centuries earlier, at the end or the latter part of the biblical period (scholars do not agree on the exact time).

Judith of the tribe of Simeon lived in the town of Bethulia, in the mountain passes along the road to Judea and Jerusalem. Nebuchadnezzar, king of Assyria, sent Holofernes, the commander of his armies, on a campaign to conquer all the lands between Assyria and Judea. When Holofernes reached Judith's town, he laid siege to it. After a month there was no water left in the town, so its leaders decided to open the town's gates and let the enemy in. Suddenly Judith, a beautiful and proud young woman of the rich Merari family came forward and asked the town's leaders for permission to go down to Holofernes' camp. They agreed, and when the Assyrian general saw her he invited her to a feast. After the meal the general, overcome by wine, fell asleep. Judith then took out his sword, cut off his head, handed it to her maid, and returned with her to the town. Deprived of their commander, the panic-stricken soldiers ran away, and Judea was saved. The Book of Judith, which did not become part of the Hebrew Bible, has been preserved in other languages and popularized in many cultures through stories, plays, and art.

Judith with the Head of Holofernes, by Lucas Cranach the Elder

A third woman of this period, Queen Salome Alexandra, is a historical figure rather than a legend. After the death of the Maccabean brothers, their offspring ruled over Judea as mon-

28

archs and high priests. Their rule was not always benevolent, nor was it peaceful. A great deal of internal strife and many wars with Israel's neighbors marked that period. The reign of Salome Alexandra, however, was a time of peace with neighboring nations and harmony between the court and the Pharisees, who were becoming the religious authority for the Jews. Salome Alexandra was a wise ruler. She did not enter into any risky alliances with neighboring nations nor seek conflicts with them, at the same time maintaining a strong army and fortifying her borders to secure peace.

The three women associated with the Maccabean period we have presented here had two things in common. First, all were courageous women, unafraid of life's challenges, to which they responded with pride and dignity. Second, all were faithful daughters of their people, to whom preserving their people and their heritage was more important than self-interest and personal gain. Finally, they were willing to make the supreme sacrifice for their people. They were truly blessed daughters of Israel.

Courtesy of the collection of Miriam Lipstadt Roth

Hanukkah menorah (eighteenth-century Poland)

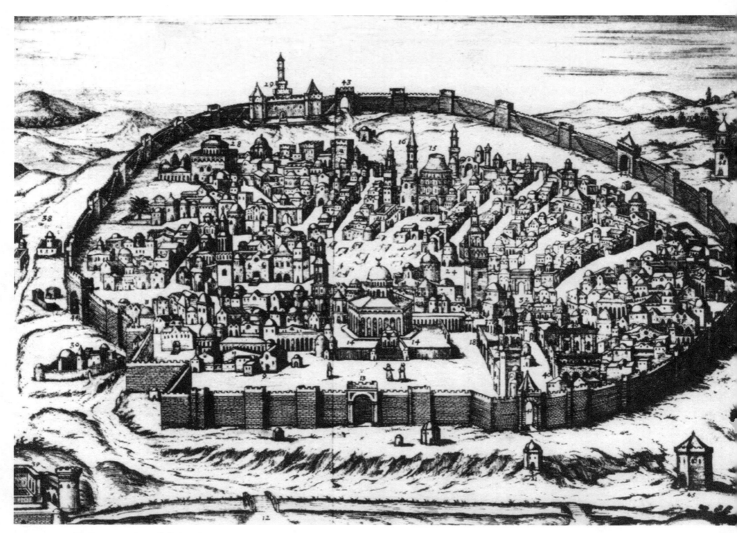

Early engraving of Jerusalem

The Holy Temple, a scale model

Chapter Four

Women in the Talmud

The biblical period and the Maccabean period which followed it had one important thing in common. During both periods, the Jewish people had their Holy Temple in Jerusalem. Originally built by King Solomon, it was destroyed by the Babylonians in 586 B.C.E. and rebuilt by the Judean exiles who returned from Babylonia seventy years later. In the year 70 C.E. it was destroyed again, this time by the Romans, and it has remained in ruins ever since (we still have the remnants of one of the walls that surrounded it, namely the Western Wall).

The Western Wall (oil painting by D. Bida)

Torah scroll, case, and crown
designed by Ludwig Y. Wolpert

*This Torah will not depart
from your mouth, and
you shall meditate upon it
day and night.*
—Joshua 1:8

After the destruction of the Temple, the Jews no longer had one central place of worship. Instead, they began to pray and study in local houses of worship which became known as "synagogues," from the Greek word meaning "house of assembly." No longer ruled by kings and queens, Jewish life was now guided by rabbis and scholars who created a large body of interpretations and stories based on the sacred text of the Bible. Around the year 500 C.E., these teachings and writings were collected in several volumes and became known as the Talmud.

The Talmud contains many statements and stories regarding the virtues and merits of women. The Bible tells us that when Moses went up to Mount Sinai to receive the Ten Commandments, the children of Israel pressured Aaron to make them a golden calf that they might worship. According to a Talmudic legend, Aaron tried to delay matters by asking for contributions of gold and silver with which to make the calf. The men responded immediately, but the women refused to give up their rings and bracelets for something they knew would anger God. They asked, "How dare we anger God, who has performed great miracles for us, freed us from slavery in Egypt, and allowed us to cross the Red Sea unharmed?"

Later, during the exodus, after the scouts whom Moses had sent to Canaan to "spy on the land" returned with the unfavorable report that the Promised Land would be impossible to conquer because it was inhabited by awesome giants, the men cried out, "Let us make a captain and let us return to Egypt." But the women, discounting the exaggerated report of the fearfulness of the inhabitants of the Promised Land, would not agree. They insisted on going forward to conquer Canaan, in accordance with the will of God.

These stories are typical of the many examples in rabbinical literature of the piety, steadfastness, and courage of women. In some places in the Talmud, however, we find uncomplimentary remarks about women. For example, women are said to be overcurious, gossipy, frivolous, and fickle—negative qualities which have been attributed to women throughout time. Yet, if you look at the totality of Talmudic and post-Talmudic statements and comments about women, you will see that Judaism has always held women in high esteem and has often attributed to them greater virtues than those associated with men.

🌿 🌿 🌿

According to the Talmud, the world stands on three things: the study of Torah, or God's word; prayer, or the worship of God; and acts of kindness, or proper behavior towards human beings, who are God's children. The Talmudic period in Jewish history shaped Judaism for the next two thousand years, putting study, prayer, and charitable acts at the center of Jewish life. With regard to charitable acts, the Talmud makes no distinction between men and women. Both are called upon to perform such acts. But study and prayer became primarily the domain of men. While women were not prevented from studying and praying, they were neither obligated nor encouraged to pursue those activities.

One Talmudic rabbi of the third century, Rabbi Eliezer, said, "He who teaches his daughter Torah is teaching her a subject for which she has neither taste nor inclination." But Rabbi Eliezer was contradicted by a contemporary rabbi, Bar Azzai, who declared, "A father is obligated to teach his daughter the Torah." It was Bar Azzai's view that prevailed—in fact, Rabbi Eliezer did not practice what he preached. He himself married a woman famous for her learning; many instances of her intelligence and knowledge are cited in the Talmud.

The Talmud contains several examples of women of great character and learning. We will mention only two. The first is Rachel, the wife of Rabbi Akiva. Thanks to her, Akiva became one of the greatest scholars and leaders in the Talmud and in all of Jewish history. The daughter of a rich landowner in the Jerusalem countryside, Rachel fell in love with Akiva, an uneducated shepherd who tended her father's flocks. Rachel's father, disapproving of the marriage, disowned her, and the young couple lived in great poverty.

The story of Rachel and her beloved Akiva is one of the greatest love stories of all time. Akiva felt guilty for having taken Rachel away from her life of comfort and affluence. We are told that he wanted to buy her a "Jerusalem of Gold," a golden comb popular in those days, but he could not afford it. Rachel did not seem to mind, since to her Akiva was more important to her than gold

Front page of the Talmud. The text is in the center, surrounded by commentary.

33

and jewelry. Moreover, Rachel recognized Akiva's great potential for scholarship and persuaded him to go at age forty to study Torah at the great academies of Babylonia. Years later Akiva returned, followed by thousands of students. When Rachel came to greet him, his students did not recognize her and tried to push her out of the greater master's way. Akiva stopped them and said, "You and I, we all owe our learning and wisdom to her."

Studying the Talmud (woodcut by Joseph Budko)

Another great woman of the Talmudic period was Bruriah, the wife of Rabbi Meir. Bruriah, a scholar in her own right, may very well be considered the first woman rabbi in history. She was also a woman of uncommon courage. The story is told that her two sons suddenly died on the Sabbath, while her husband was in the synagogue. When Rabbi Meir came home and gave her the Sabbath greeting, she decided to wait until the end of the holy day to break the terrible news to him, rather than turn his Sabbath into mourning. She put a bed sheet over her sons' bodies, and when Rabbi Meir asked her where the boys were, she told him they had gone to the House of Study. He told her he had stopped there earlier but had not seen them. Bruriah gave him the wine cup for the Havdalah, the prayer ending the Sabbath, and told him to proceed.

After the prayer, Rabbi Meir asked again for his sons. Bruriah told him that they had gone elsewhere and would be back soon. She gave him his supper, and he said the blessing. After he finished she told him that someone had once given her something for safekeeping, and had just come back to claim it. Should she give it back? He said to her, "Of course, my dear. You must return it." She took him by the hand and led him to the room where he saw his sons lying on the bed, lifeless. As he began to cry and wail for his beloved sons, Bruriah calmed him and said, "The Lord gave and the Lord took back. Blessed be the name of the Lord." She was able to overcome her grief and accept the divine decree, and she helped her husband, a great rabbi, follow her example.

34

Chapter Five

Exemplary Women under Cross and Crescent

In the second century C.E., during the lifetime of Rachel and Bruriah, the Jews in the Land of Israel made their last valiant attempt to become a free people. Inspired by the aging Rabbi Akiva, the warrior Shimon Bar Kokhba overthrew Roman rule for a period of two years. But small Judea was no match for the mighty Roman Empire. When the best Roman legions were brought in to crush the rebellion, close to half a million Jews were massacred, Jerusalem was razed, its name was changed to Aelia Capitolina, and Jews were forbidden to live in their holy city. This was in effect the beginning of eighteen centuries of Jewish statelessness, during which time Jews lived as a persecuted people wandering from country to country, always at the whim and mercy of the local ruler.

The Destruction of Jerusalem (oil by Bernard Picart, 1712)

During that time Christianity became the dominant religion of Europe, and about one hundred years after the end of the Talmudic period, in the seventh century, a new religion named Islam emerged and took over much of the Middle East, North Africa, and parts of Europe. The mission of both Christians and Muslims was to convert all those they came in contact with to their own faith, which they believed to be the only true faith. As a result, Jews did not fare well under either host religion, both in the Middle East and in Europe. Jews turned more and more inward, living separately from their surrounding cultures, sustained by their rich spiritual heritage embodied in the Hebrew Bible and

Doña Gracia Nasi (with a view of the Sea of Galilee)

Talmudic law and lore. The Jewish family became the mainstay of Jewish life, and the synagogue became the center of every Jewish community, large and small.

By the end of the first millennium of our Common Era, the center of Jewish life had shifted from east to west. The great Talmudic academies of Palestine and Babylonia were replaced by new centers of Jewish life and learning in Spain, at that time under Islamic rule. Despite many ups and downs, Jewish life in Spain under Islam was one of the high points in Jewish history. Great Jewish philosophers like Maimonides enriched Jewish and general learning, and great poets like Yehuda Ha-Levi made major contributions to Hebrew literature. Jews excelled in all areas of human knowledge and endeavor, and in the late fifteenth century were instrumental in helping Columbus discover the New World.

This glorious era ended in 1492—the year Columbus discovered America—when the Catholic King Ferdinand and Queen Isabella completed the conquest of Spain and, urged by the Spanish Inquisition, expelled all the Jews from Spain. Some Jews found refuge in nearby Portugal and Italy, while others migrated as far east as Germany and Poland. A new time of hardship and persecution began.

Over the next two centuries, at least two remarkable women left their mark on our people's history. One was a direct descendant of Spanish Jews, the other a German Jewish woman who lived a century later.

The first was Doña Gracia Nasi, born in Portugal about eighteen years after the expulsion of the Jews from Spain. Like many of the Jews of Spain and Portugal at that time, her family was forced to convert to Christianity, becoming what were known as Marrano Jews, a derogatory term applied during the Spanish Inquisition to Jews who outwardly embraced the Christian faith but secretly continued to observe the laws and rituals of Judaism. Doña Gracia was baptized at birth and named Beatrice.

As Beatrice grew up, however, her great desire was to return to her ancestral Jewish faith and practice it openly. At age eighteen she married a rich merchant named Francisco Mendes, also a Marrano Jew. Trading in precious stones, Mendes and his brother Diego built a banking network which extended to London and to Antwerp, Belgium. When Beatrice turned twenty-six, her husband died, and she found herself alone with her young daughter, Reyna, her sister, also named Reyna, and her two young nephews, Joseph and Samuel, the sons of her late brother.

No longer feeling safe in Portugal, Beatrice took the three children, her sister, and most of her fortune and escaped to England. Not comfortable there either, she continued to Antwerp, where she joined her brother-in-law, Diego, who by now had become one of the most powerful traders in the city. It was in Antwerp that this remarkable young woman began her amazing career not only as a highly successful business-woman, but also as a Jewish leader who sought to restore Jewish dignity and freedom.

Made a full partner by Diego, Beatrice became a familiar figure among the upper class of the city. Soon she began to help her brother-in-law in his efforts to aid fellow Marrano Jews escape from Portugal. At the same time, the two of them contacted the Pope in Rome and asked that he stop the activities of the Inquisition in Italy. Their efforts were partially successful.

But Beatrice's greatest wish continued to be a full return to Judaism, which was not possible in Antwerp. She tried to convince her brother-in-law to relocate the family business, but he refused. She finally decided to go it alone and had started preparing for her departure when Diego suddenly died. He left her all the assets and operations of the Mendes banking house, making her, at age thirty-two, the head of the Mendes family.

Taking as many of the assets as she could, Beatrice left Antwerp and settled in Venice. There she encountered new troubles, this time caused not by the Church or the secular authorities, but by her own sister, who opposed her plans of returning to Judaism and possibly moving to Turkey, where she could finally live openly as a Jew. Beatrice was denounced to the authorities by her sister, who accused her of breaking the law of the land by bringing people back to Judaism. Through Turkish diplomatic intervention, however, Beatrice was able to leave Venice and settle in the Italian city of Ferrara.

It was there that Beatrice Luna finally was able to return to Judaism. She changed her name to Gracia Nasi, using the original Hebrew name of her family. In Ferrara she helped rescue hundreds of Marrano Jews from Portugal and became known as a leader of Spanish and Portuguese Jews and as the

Medal dated 1553 with the words "Gracia Nasi" in Hebrew

most important Jewish woman of her time. Her face appeared on medals inscribed with her name in Hebrew. Jewish scholars dedicated their work to her, including a Spanish translation of the Bible (the 1553 Ferrara Spanish Bible) that sustained Marrano Jews for many years.

Doña Gracia did not stay long in Ferrara. Coming full circle from the time her ancestors flourished in Spain under Islam, she settled in Constantinople, the Turkish capital and the center of the Islamic world at that time. The Ottoman Empire under Suleiman the Magnificent was at the peak of its power, and Suleiman was one of the most enlightened rulers in Islamic history. Doña Gracia prospered in the Turkish capital, and her efforts on behalf of her fellow Jews increased. She became the patron of the Jewish communities of Turkey, mainly in Constantinople and Salonika. She organized help for the poor, financed schools and synagogues, and supported Jewish scholars. Her nephew openly embraced Judaism, took on the Hebrew name Joseph Nasi, and married her daughter, Reyna. He became Doña Gracia's partner in all her commercial activities, which were far-reaching.

While basking in the sun of her new homeland, Doña Gracia did not forget her Marrano brothers and sisters. When Pope Paul IV burned twenty-six Marrano Jews at the stake in the Italian port city of Ancona, she organized a boycott of the city and arranged for the Turkish sultan to intervene on behalf of the Jews of Ancona, who were Turkish subjects.

Auto-da-fé—the burning of Jews by the Church (fifteenth-century woodcut)

This remarkable Jewish woman died at the age of forty-nine. During the last three years of her life, she embarked on the most ambitious project in her lifelong pursuit of restoring dignity and freedom to her people. She had reached the same conclusion which Jews would reach again years later, in our own time: The only place where Jews could once again live free from persecution was their own ancestral land, the Land of Israel. She petitioned the sultan and was allowed to lease the town of Tiberias in northern Israel, on the shore of the Sea of Galilee, along with several surrounding villages. She built a wall around Tiberias to protect its residents, and established a residence for herself and a Talmudic academy.

It is not clear whether Doña Gracia actually settled in Tiberias. But since no records show that she lived in Constantinople at that time, it is entirely possible that she did spend time in Tiberias and even died there. Thus, Doña Gracia may be considered the first Zionist leader who sought to bring the Jews back to their homeland. She was certainly a blessed daughter of her people, and one of the most remarkable women in all of Jewish history.

❦ ❦ ❦

Some seventy years after the time of Doña Gracia Nasi, another Jewish woman, Glueckel of Hameln, left her mark on the history of her people. Unlike her illustrious predecessor, Glueckel did not assume the role of a communal or political leader. She was a very private person who attended to her family and helped her husband in his business. But her name would reach us because of her diary, which proved invaluable for studying Jewish life at that time.

By the mid-seventeenth century, the center of Jewish life began to shift from the Mediterranean to Central and Eastern Europe. The Jews of Spain who had spread throughout the Mediterranean countries and the Middle East became known as Sephardim (from the Hebrew word *Sepharad*, meaning Spain). Depending on where they lived, they spoke either Ladino, a Judeo-Spanish dialect, or Judeo-Arabic. The Jews of Germany spoke a Judeo-German dialect which in time became known as Yiddish.

Glueckel was born in Hamburg, Germany to a prominent family. At a young age she was exposed to hardship and persecution when her family was expelled from Hamburg and forced to settle in nearby Altona, Denmark while her father stayed in Hamburg to pursue his trade. Hard times did not prevent Glueckel from pursuing both Jewish and secular studies, and she became learned in both at a young age.

When she was fourteen she married Haim of Hameln. The young couple moved back to Hamburg, where Glueckel became her husband's adviser in all business matters while also raising a family of twelve children. Glueckel would later describe her thirty years of marriage to her first husband as the happiest years of her life. When he died, she took full charge of his business and continued to raise and marry off her children. To cope with loneliness, and anxious to preserve the family history for her children and grandchildren, she began to keep a diary.

Glueckel was a keen observer of her surroundings, and a very skillful and sensitive writer. She described in great detail

Glueckel of Hameln

The best thing for you, my dear children, is to serve God from your heart, without falsehood or sham.
—Glueckel of Hameln

39

Passover cup (Germany,
seventeenth century)

life in Hamburg, Berlin, and Amsterdam. What becomes clear from reading her diary is that life for most people in her day was harsh, and life for the Jews, who were constantly mistreated and often assaulted and expelled from their homes and country of residence, was doubly difficult. But what is most remarkable about Glueckel's diary is that its author never lost her sweet disposition, was always able to find inspiration in her Jewish faith, and managed to see the positive side of every situation.

The most important thing about Glueckel's diary is the portrait it offers us of a Jewish woman who lived three hundred years ago. It helps us understand the role women played in those days in keeping their families together, providing both sustenance and education for their children, and keeping a strong faith in Jewish tradition and the teachings of Judaism. In her diary, Glueckel advises her children to always maintain a strong faith in the Almighty, and to always strive to live a life of honesty and integrity as the best weapon against evil. Rather than preach to her children, she always shows the way by personal example.

In this chapter we have seen two very different women. One was a great leader, the other a very private woman. Yet the two had a great deal in common. Both had to face great adversity because of their Jewish faith, and both were able to overcome it. Not only did adversity fail to weaken their Jewish faith, it actually reinforced it. Out of Jewish tradition they drew the courage and inspiration to live productive lives which brought them fulfillment and enriched the lives of those they touched. In her own way, each was a truly blessed daughter of Israel.

Chapter Six

Emancipation and the New World

People have always yearned for freedom and equality. But much of the freedom and equality many of us enjoy today has come about only in recent generations. The post-Medieval world of Gracia Nasi and Glueckel of Hameln was not a place where monarchs and the state religion offered people freedom and equality. People had no say as to who governed them, had very few rights and opportunities, and were for the most part happy to be left alone and spared the ravages of armed conflict and oppression.

All this began to change in the late eighteenth century, thanks to two related events. The first was the American Revolution in 1776, and the second was the French Revolution in 1789. Those two events provided the momentum for creating freedom and equality in the Western world. For the Jews, however, the process was much slower. For one thing, Jews were not considered citizens of their countries of residence until later in the nineteenth century (in Russia not until after the Russian Revolution in 1917). As aliens in their own native countries, they had to struggle to become citizens, and once they had become citizens they were not considered fully equal. The period during which Jews sought acceptance as citizens and as equal members of society is known in Jewish history as the time of the Emancipation.

Wooden synagogue in Poland, early nineteenth century

During the time of the Emancipation, some remarkable Jewish women made major contributions to Jewish life and

41

Rebecca Gratz (painting by Thomas Sully, from the collection of Henrietta Clay)

It is not too much to hope, too much to expect from the daughters of a noble race that they will be foremost in the work of charity.
—Rebecca Gratz

to society as a whole, both in Europe and in the New World. In this chapter we will look at four of these women, two in the United States and two in Europe. In her own way, each transcended the restrictions imposed on women in general and on Jewish women in particular, making unique contributions to her own people and to society at large.

The first of these women was Rebecca Gratz, undoubtedly the most remarkable Jewish woman in nineteenth-century America. One of the most endearing characters in English literature, Rebecca—the daughter of Isaac of York in Sir Walter Scott's famous novel *Ivanhoe*—was supposedly modeled after Rebecca Gratz. Everything else we know about her life and her accomplishments is carefully documented fact.

When Rebecca grew up after the American Revolution in late eighteenth-century Philadelphia, the city had a few hundred Jewish residents. Jewish life centered around the city's first synagogue, Mikveh Israel, where Rebecca's father, the wealthy merchant Michael Gratz, was a lay leader. In Rebecca's time, many of the American Jewish institutions which make American Jewry the best organized Jewish community in the world did not exist. During her long life, Rebecca would make an enormous contribution towards organizing some of those key institutions.

The Gratzes, who belonged to the top social circles in the city, did not spare any effort in providing the best education for their children, boys and girls alike. In fact, Rebecca's older sister Richea was the first woman in America to attend college. Rebecca herself did not go to college, but she did acquire a great deal of knowledge on her own. She grew up in a traditional Jewish home which was strictly kosher, and from a young age Rebecca displayed a strong allegiance to her Jewish roots. Still, she felt equally at home in the non-Jewish society of Philadelphia. Her closest friend in her teens was Maria Fenno, a non-Jew. When a yellow fever epidemic broke out in Philadelphia in 1798 and Maria lost her parents, Rebecca learned firsthand about bereavement and the plight of orphans. This experience would affect the future course of her life.

In her late teens, Rebecca took her place among the city's social and literary elite. She knew some of the important American leaders, writers, and artists of the day, including Henry Clay, Washington Irving, and the painter Thomas Sully, who painted her famous portrait. She corresponded with leading women writers of her time, such as British educator and novelist Maria Edgeworth, American author Catherine Sedgwick,

British actress Fanny Kemble, and Jewish-British theologian Grace Aguilar. Rebecca's friends encouraged her to submit her own poetry to a literary magazine, but she refused. She was never interested in fame. Instead, she used her writing to correspond and to develop organizational reports as part of her many endeavors on behalf of the common good.

As a young woman, Gratz did not engage in romantic pursuits. She remained single for the rest of her life. She had a brief romance with a prominent Christian minister's son but refused him when he proposed to her. It appears that she wanted to marry a fellow Jew and create a Jewish home, and we can only speculate that there were few eligible Jewish bachelors in America at that time. Her portraits reveal a rare and radiant beauty, and her nobility of character is confirmed by her actions and her writings.

In 1801, together with her mother, sister, and twenty-one other prominent women, Gratz founded Philadelphia's first nonsectarian women's charitable organization, the Female Association for the Relief of Women and Children in Reduced Circumstances. This organization became a model for many similar organizations in which women took full charge. Gratz became the organization's secretary because of her skills as a writer. In this position for twenty-one years, she took minutes, handled correspondence, authored annual reports, and wrote other public documents for the organization.

By the time Gratz turned thirty, she had lost both her parents and a sister who left behind nine orphans. She assumed responsibility for her nieces and nephews and also for her unmarried brothers, Hyman, Joseph, and Jacob, becoming in effect the matriarch of her family. Following her example, her brothers became active in both Jewish and nonsectarian cultural and charitable organizations in the city, including the Chestnut Street Theater and the Deaf and Dumb Home.

Philadelphia, early nineteenth century

Gratz's experience with the Female Association and the Philadelphia Orphan Asylum led her to believe that Jewish women were especially equipped to take care of the greater "house of Israel," namely, the Jewish community at large. Because her work with nonsectarian charitable organizations had convinced her that even the most well-meaning Christians were often eager to convert others, she became concerned about the growing number of needy Philadelphia Jews. In 1819 she helped establish the Female Hebrew Benevolent Society. This organization provided Philadelphia's impoverished Jews with

Burning of the Philadelphia Orphan Asylum

food, clothing, fuel, and other necessities. It was the first non-synagogue-centered Jewish women's organization in America. Again she served as secretary, a position she held nearly forty years. She was intent on bolstering the status of women in the community and showing that Jews could take care of their own.

Through her communal work, Gratz gained community respect and admiration, becoming an important figure in her own right. At the same time, she became increasingly concerned about the lack of Jewish education for her own relatives and for the Jewish community as a whole. In those days, Bar Mitzvah preparation and private tutoring were the only types of formal Jewish education available for boys, and there was none at all for girls. At the same time, Christian denominations in the United States were becoming more and more active, and the Christian Sunday School movement was gaining momentum. It became clear to Gratz that future generations of American Jews faced rapid assimilation unless Jewish education became more accessible.

In 1838, on her fifty-seventh birthday, Gratz opened the first Jewish Sunday school in America, with sixty students enrolled. With no textbooks and no curriculum, she had to borrow Christian Bibles and create her own lesson plans. The school was coeducational and run entirely by women. Classes met only once a week and were taught in English. It was the first Jewish institution in America to give women a public role in the education of Jewish children. The model spread quickly to cities like Charleston, Savannah, and Baltimore and in time became the model for the leading Jewish school systems in America, particularly that of Reform Judaism.

In her seventies, Gratz organized the Jewish Foster Home, the first Jewish orphanage in North America. It took in children from all over the United States and Canada. At age seventy-four she became secretary of the home. For several more years, she continued to serve in that capacity while sitting on the boards of the Female Hebrew Benevolent Society and the Philadelphia Orphan Asylum, and serving as superintendent of the Hebrew Sunday School.

Gratz was eighty when the Civil War broke out in 1861. She strongly opposed slavery and found herself in a difficult situation because her relatives were scattered throughout the North and South and held opposing views on the issue. She tried to maintain contact with and counsel them all but was not able to reconcile their opposing views. She wrote to her sister-in-law: "I have been reading some loving letters from some so near to me in blood and affections whose arms are perhaps now raised against those hearts at which they have fed."

Gratz was eighty-eight when she died in 1869. The social welfare and educational institutions she created became models for American society and American Jewry and have had a far-reaching impact on both. Historian Diane Ashton wrote, "By training younger Jewish women in administering the agencies she founded, Gratz ensured that the FHBS and JFH would continue to flourish long after her death. In their work, these organizations continued to provide Jewish women and children a way to be both fully Jewish and fully American."

The year Rebecca Gratz passed away, a young Jewish woman turned twenty in New York City. Her name was Emma Lazarus. We remember her mainly because of a poem she wrote in honor of the Statue of Liberty, built in France to commemorate the American Revolution and dedicated in New York in 1886, the year before Lazarus died at age thirty-eight. This poem, titled "The New Colossus," became one of the best known and loved expressions of the United States as a haven for the persecuted and a land of opportunity for people from all over the world:

> Not like the brazen giant of Greek fame
> With conquering limbs astride from land to land;
> Here at our sea-washed, sunset gates shall stand
> A mighty woman with a torch, whose flame
> Is the imprisoned lightning, and her name
> Mother of Exiles. From her beacon-hand
> Glows world-wide welcome; her mild eyes command
> The air-bridged harbor that twin cities frame.
> "Keep, ancient lands, your storied pomp!" cries she
> With silent lips. "Give me your tired, your poor
> Your huddled masses yearning to breathe free,
> The wretched refuse of your teeming shore.
> Send these, the homeless, tempest-tossed to me,
> I lift my lamp beside the golden door!"

Emma Lazarus

There was a great deal more to Emma Lazarus than this one poem. Her ancestors came to America long before the American Revolution, escaping the Inquisition in Spain. By the mid-nineteenth century, the small Spanish-Jewish community of New York had become part of the Jewish upper

The Statue of Liberty, New York Harbor

Give me your tired, your poor,
Your huddlled masses yearning
to breathe free.
—Emma Lazarus

class. Emma was raised in a comfortable home and studied with private tutors. At an early age, she showed great interest in classic literature and modern languages. When she turned eighteen she published her first book of poems, which attracted the attention of the foremost literary figure in America at that time, Ralph Waldo Emerson. Four years later she dedicated her second volume of poetry to him. In this volume she included her first poem on a Jewish theme, "In the Jewish Synagogue in Newport."

Emerson encouraged Lazarus to continue writing, and she turned to writing historical novels. Lazarus was inspired by the great English novelist George Eliot (a pseudonym for Mary Ann Evans), who was sympathetic to the plight of the Jews in Europe. Eliot's novel *Daniel Deronda* contains a call for a Jewish national revival.

In those years—the late nineteenth century—the first waves of Jewish immigrants began arriving in America from Russia. The old Spanish and German Jewish communities of New York looked down on their poor, unsophisticated brothers and sisters escaping pogroms in the Old Country. Lazarus defended Russian Jews in her writings, foreshadowing her famous poem about "huddled masses yearning to breathe free."

Like Rebecca Gratz before her, Lazarus realized that the future of the Jewish people was in jeopardy, and something had to be done about it. She began to dedicate her time and energy to translating the great Spanish-Jewish poets, including Yehuda Ha-Levi and Solomon ibn Gabirol. She also advocated a national revival of Jewish life and culture in the Holy Land and in America, which in effect made her an early Zionist. She wrote:

> *Wake, Israel, wake! Recall today the glorious Maccabean*
> *rage,*
> *Oh, deem not dead that martial fire, say not the mystic*
> *flame is spent!*
> *With Moses' law and David's lyre, your ancient strength*
> *remains unbent,*
> *Let but an Ezra rise anew, to lift the banner of the Jew!*

Like Gratz in her charitable work, Lazarus demonstrated in her writing that one could be dedicated both to Jewish and American ideals, which are complementary. Lazarus was admired as both a Jewish and an American writer by such great American contemporary poets as Henry Wadsworth Longfellow and Walt Whitman.

46

When the Statue of Liberty arrived in New York in 1885, funds had to be raised to build a huge pedestal in the middle of New York Harbor, where this gigantic statue would stand as a symbol of hope for arriving immigrants. Writers and artists in New York, including Longfellow, Whitman, and Mark Twain, were invited to contribute their work to the fund-raising effort. Lazarus was also invited to contribute, but at first she refused, arguing that she could not write on order. Inspired, however, by the plight of the Russian refugees, she wrote "The New Colossus." An unheard of sum of $21,500 was raised for this one short poem, which to this day has remained one of America's favorites.

After her premature death, when Lazarus' collected poems were being published, her sister objected to including any poem with a Jewish subject. This would have greatly displeased Lazarus. History, however, has proven her right, as her two life's dreams became a reality in the next century: her American dream of huddled masses of immigrants becoming integrated in American society, and her Jewish dream of a persecuted people once again becoming a free nation in their own land.

Rebecca Gratz and Emma Lazarus had two contemporaries in Europe, both of whom were most unusual daughters of Israel and also left their mark on the Jewish world and on Western culture. The lives and careers of these two women—a Hasidic rabbi and a French actress—represent two extremes. The first, known as the Maid of Ludomir, was the first and so far the only Hasidic woman rabbi. The second, Sarah Bernhardt, was the world's most acclaimed actress in the late nineteenth and early twentieth centuries.

Little is known about Hannah Rachel Werbermacher, popularly known as the Maid of Ludomir. She was born around 1805 in Ludomir, Ukraine into the world of the Hasidim, pious Jews who believe in worshiping God through joy, ecstatic prayer, fervent faith, and deep piety. The Hasidic movement began in the mid-eighteenth century as a group of sects, each devoted to its religious leader, or *rebbe*. The *rebbe* was considered a *tzaddik*, or righteous person who had achieved a high rank of holiness. Each *tzaddik* established a dynasty, whereby his son would take over as leader of the sect after his death and in turn be replaced by his own son. Some Hasidic dynasties exist to this day.

Polish Hasidic couple, *circa* 1850

When Hasidism first started in Eastern Europe in the second half of the eighteenth century, it was a revolutionary movement. The majority of the world's Jews in those days lived in the rural areas of Central and Eastern Europe, and most of them were extremely poor, living a bleak and hopeless life. Jewish learning was limited to a privileged class led by rabbis who looked down on the masses of poor and largely ignorant Jews. Founded by Rabbi Israel, or the *Baal Shem Tov* ("He of the Good Name"), Hasidism was a folk movement which insisted that a person with a pure and kind heart yet with little learning was more important in the eyes of God than one who possessed great learning. The movement kindled new hope in the hearts of thousands of Jews and grew quickly.

Tefillin cases in engraved silver, nineteenth century Poland

In his luminous book *The Romance of Hasidism*, Rabbi Jacob Minkin writes about the place of women in the early Hasidic movement. If to many of us today the Hasidic movement appears extremely old-fashioned and restrictive of women, we may be surprised to find out in reading the following lines that it actually started out granting women equality they did not enjoy in the Jewish community of those days:

> Hasidism claims the credit for having emancipated the Jewish woman. In truth, not a few women played quite an important part in the Hasidic sect both as followers and as leaders. While Rabbinism subordinated the place and position of woman to that of man and made her the inactive member of the Jewish community, Hasidism assigned to her a place and importance almost equal to that of her male partner. Rabbi Israel always spoke tenderly of his wife; when she died, he refused to remarry, remembering her loyalty and devotion in the days of their obscurity and poverty. Similar tenderness to their wives is to be found in the attitude of other Hasidic leaders. Udel, the daughter of the *Baal Shem*, enjoyed a reputation and influence in Hasidism in her own right, as did her daughter, Feige, the mother of Nahman of Bratzlav, whose gifts she helped to develop more than her husband, R. Simha, who was quite an ordinary and mediocre man. The "Maid of Ludomir" enjoyed a standing in the Hasidic sect almost equal to her counterpart in the Christian Church, having conducted herself like a *tzaddik*, with a synagogue and following all her own.

Sarah Bernhardt
THE POSTERS

Posters advertising Sarah Bernhardt's plays. The one on the left contains God's name in Hebrew. The middle one represents one of Bernhardt's greatest hits. *La Tosca* (right), better known as an opera, was one of her greatest roles.

Needlework sampler
by Rose Neuberger,
Germany (1862)

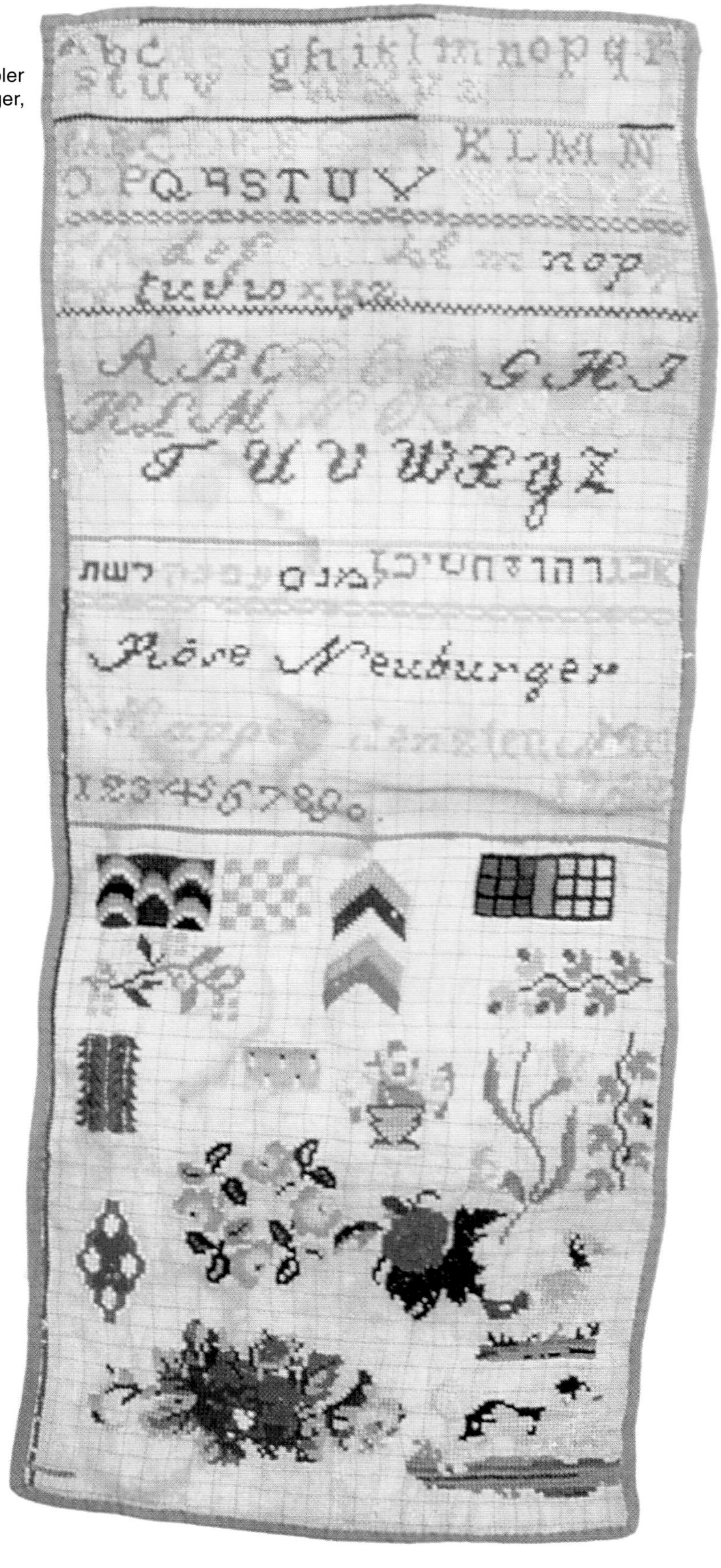

From the collections of the Judah L. Magnes Museum. Photo by Ben Ailes

It was unheard of—and still is—among the Hasidim to have a woman assume the role of *rebbe* or *tzaddik*. But this did not seem to deter Hannah Rachel from doing exactly that. At a young age she became known for her deep faith and piety. Her father saw to it that she learned Torah like a boy, and she excelled in all studies, taking a special interest in the Midrash, or lore of Judaism, and in Musar, the ethical teachings. After she turned twelve, her father wanted to find her a bright yeshiva student who would become her husband. But Hannah Rachel insisted she would choose her own mate when she was ready. She spent her days studying, and she would stand in one place and pray for hours. Some of the great *rebbes* of nearby communities heard about her piety and made attempts to find a learned husband for her. No doubt they considered her to be like Rachel, Rabbi Akiva's wife, or Bruriah, Rabbi Meir's wife. Surely she would be a great asset to some young scholar, and, who knows, their marriage might produce great scholars who would bring honor and glory to their people. Hannah Rachel, however, chose to remain single.

When her mother died she became depressed and refused to go out, except for her daily visit to her mother's grave. According to legend, on one such visit she began to cry uncontrollably and, exhausted, fell asleep in the graveyard. When she woke up she became scared of the shadows and sounds of the graveyard and started to run. She fell into a partially dug grave and fainted. Someone heard her and brought her home. She went into shock, was unable to speak for days, and nearly died. When she finally recovered, she told her father she had gone to heaven where she saw the divine throne, and was given a new and sublime soul.

Tallit

She began to wear a *tallit*, or prayer shawl, and *tefillin*, or prayer boxes, which were worn only by men. She followed all religious laws like a man. When her father died, she said *Kaddish* for him every day, a prayer reserved for a son.

Hannah Rachel became known as a holy woman and a healer, and she began to attract followers who helped her build her own synagogue. During the Third Meal on Sabbath afternoons, the door to her room leading into the synagogue would open, and she would speak words of Torah to her Hasidim.

Eventually, at age forty, she agreed to get married. Once she was married, she seemed to have lost her spark, and her

49

followers lost interest in her. She was divorced and eventually immigrated to the Land of Israel, where she spent her days engaged in mystical studies and rituals designed to hasten the coming of the Messiah. According to legend, at one point she almost succeeded in bringing the Messiah, but the meeting she had arranged during which the Messiah was expected to appear was foiled by a mysterious stranger who turned out to be Elijah the Prophet. Elijah, the one in Jewish tradition who is expected to usher in the Messiah, had apparently decided the time was not ripe for this to happen.

The Maid of Ludomir was part of a mystical tradition in Judaism, an important aspect not only of the Hasidic movement, but also of Judaism in general, going all the way back to the Bible. More relevant to our time, she was an early example in the modern world of a woman functioning as a rabbi. About one hundred years later, several non-Orthodox Jewish religious movements in the United States would open the door for women to become rabbis. And even among the Orthodox movements, which have been resisting such a change, the question is being raised today as to why women should not be allowed to serve as spiritual leaders. Those who support the change point to historical examples such as Bruriah in the Talmud and, more recently, the Maid of Ludomir.

In 1844, while Hannah Rachel was still the beloved leader of her Hasidim in Ludomir, a daughter was born out of wedlock to Judith Van Hard, a Dutch-Jewish music teacher and courtesan living in Paris. The child was named Rosine, but she would become known to the world as Sarah Bernhardt. Years later, adoring audiences would call her "the divine Sarah."

The world of Sarah Bernhardt was the total opposite of that of Hannah Rachel Werbermacher. In the late nineteenth century, Paris was the cultural capital of the enlightened world. While the Jewish masses of Eastern Europe were living in great poverty and suffering extreme discrimination under the Czar, they looked upon Paris—as did the rest of the world—as the source of progress in all fields.

Paris attracted the greatest creative spirits of the day—both French and foreign—and among them were Jews like the great German poet Heinrich Heine and the painter Camille Pissarro, who influenced the great Impressionist painters. But great artists like Heine and Pissarro paid a price for becoming part of West-

Sarah Bernhardt

ern culture. They had to turn their backs on their Jewish origins since Paris, despite its passion for justice and equality, did not seem ready to include the Jews in its progressive vision.

From a young age, Bernhardt had to fend for herself. Her mother had little time for her, and she was raised in a convent. Although proud of her Jewish origins, she considered becoming a nun. Showing a talent for acting, however, she was accepted as a drama student at the French state drama school.

In her teens, Bernhardt was a restless, free spirit. She did not apply herself to her drama lessons, and her teachers did not consider her a good prospect for the stage. She did, however, manage to get a part in the *Comédie Française's* production of Racine's *Iphigénie en Aulide*, but her acting did not elicit much praise. Later, her temper got her fired from the company when she slapped a senior actress.

Bernhardt began to doubt her acting talent but continued to act in other companies. Soon, her rich voice and striking presence began to attract attention, and she was on her way to becoming the greatest stage actress of her time.

When the Germans laid siege on Paris in 1870, Bernhardt turned the Odéon Theater, where she acted, into a military hospital. Around that time she was discovered by the great French writer Victor Hugo, author of *Les Misérables*. Hugo was so taken with her acting, he called her "the divine Sarah." The name stuck.

Rehired by the *Comédie Française*, Bernhardt became France's leading actress. Unable to accept authority, however, she broke her contract and became an independent actress, starting her own company. She began the world tours which brought her fame and fortune. Everywhere she went—in Europe, the United States, and Latin America—she was received by adoring audiences. She was one of the first superstars of modern times. She was greeted by royalty and showered with furs and jewelry by admiring fans. Often on her world tours she would hear antisemitic remarks, and her response was always, "I, too, am a daughter of the great Jewish people!"

In the history of the theater, few names are as revered as that of Sarah Bernhardt. In her seventies she played the role of a teenager. When she died, she was at work on a new form of performing art, motion pictures.

French stamp with Sarah Bernhardt

I, too, am a daughter of the great Jewish people!
—Sarah Bernhardt

51

Bernhardt in one of her roles

Sarah Bernhardt was much more than an actress. In late nineteenth-century France she was a cultural institution. She was also a daughter of Israel who knew great misery and great success. In a world that was hostile toward Jews, she remained proud of her heritage. Living in a city that during her lifetime would stage the most famous antisemitic trial of history, the court martial of Alfred Dreyfus, she was a constant reminder to those who sought to blame the Jews for all of France's problems that a Jewish woman of humble origins could bring glory to their country.

We have looked at four remarkable women who lived during the nineteenth century, the time known in Jewish history as the Emancipation. In many ways, these women have served as a model and an inspiration to twentieth-century Jewish women who have made great contributions to the Jewish people and to the world. In looking at great Jewish women in the twentieth century, especially during the last third of the century, we will see that women have made significant contributions in practically every area of human endeavor.

Chapter Seven

Early Twentieth Century

In Jewish history, the twentieth century may be considered the most important century since biblical times. The two key events of this century, which surpass anything that happened to Jews during the previous twenty centuries, were the Holocaust and the birth of the State of Israel. If you were to ask which Jewish woman played the most important role in the early twentieth century in shaping the course of Jewish history during that century, the answer would probably be Henrietta Szold. Her two key contributions were founding the Hadassah organization and organizing Youth Aliyah.

Szold was born in Baltimore in 1860. Her father, Rabbi Benjamin Szold, was a scholar and leader of Conservative Judaism. Rabbi Szold guided his daughter's education, and from early youth Henrietta became a companion and assistant to her father in his complex tasks. She grew up in an environment of sympathy and understanding for all manner of human beings. In her home she became acquainted with the movement to liberate the former slaves. When Eastern European Jewish immigrants poured into America, the Szolds provided shelter, aid, and guidance to all within its reach. While teaching at a fashionable girls' school, Szold founded, managed, and taught in one of the first schools for immigrants in the United States.

Szold shared her father's scholarly interests and wrote articles for periodicals at the young age of seventeen. When the Jewish Publication Society of America was organized in 1888, she became a volunteer member of its publication committee, and from 1893 to 1916 she was its paid literary secretary. Her translation labors in this capacity included editing a five-volume translation of Heinrich Gratz's *History of the Jews.* She also translated and edited the seven-volume *Legends of the Jews* by Louis Ginzberg. In addition, together with Cyrus Adler she edited *The American Jewish Year Book.*

Szold's Zionism developed naturally out of her home atmosphere and was nourished by her scholarly preoccupation with Jewish history and literature. In 1895 Szold made her first Zionist speech before the Baltimore section of the National Council of Jewish Women. In 1909 she traveled to Europe with her mother. The trip included a visit to Palestine, where Szold wrote, "If not Zionism, then nothing," and, "There are heroic men and women here doing valiant work. If only they could be more intelligently supported by the European and American Jews." She was deeply disturbed by the lack of health care and medical services in Palestine, where many suffered from diseases such as malaria. Upon her return to the United States, she decided it was her duty to do something about it. In 1912 Szold approached the Hadassah Study Circle, to which she had belonged since 1907, and offered to transform it into a national women's organization that would raise funds for health care in Palestine. The name of the new organization was quite appropriate. "Hadassah" is the Hebrew name of Queen Esther, the woman who saved the Jewish people from the wicked Haman in biblical times. Hadassah's first goal, to establish a network of visiting nurses, began modestly in 1913 with the arrival of two American-trained nurses who set up a small welfare station in Jerusalem.

Henrietta Szold

If not Zionism, then nothing.
—Henrietta Szold

That same year, Szold began a series of U.S. tours for Hadassah. The organization grew in strength and membership. During World War I, Supreme Court Justice Louis D. Brandeis, head of the Provisional Zionist Committee, entrusted Szold with the responsibility of organizing the American Zionist Medical Unit for Palestine. In the fall of 1918, equipment for a fifty-bed hospital and a group of forty-four doctors, nurses, dentists, sanitary engineers, and administrators arrived in Palestine. Szold joined them in 1920, and from then until 1927, she divided her time between Hadassah's work in Palestine and in the U.S. Even after she had settled permanently in Palestine and undertaken other major responsibilities, she remained dedicated to Hadassah. In 1926, she was elected honorary president of the organization. In 1933, she laid the foundation stone for the Rothschild Hadassah University Hospital. When World War II broke out, she served on the Hadassah Emergency Committee engaged in solving the problems created by the war. Based on Szold's survey and recommendations, Hadassah established the Alice Seligsberg Trade School for Girls in Jerusalem.

In 1927, Szold was elected one of the three members of the Palestine Executive Committee of the World Zionist Organization. She was the first woman ever to serve in this capacity, and her portfolios included education and health. However, since the two other members of the committee (Harry Sacher and Colonel Frederick Kisch) were frequently abroad for long periods, the task of political work and negotiations with Palestine's government on behalf of the *yishuv* (Jewish Community) fell upon her. The prevailing attitude toward women at that time made Szold's work more difficult. The *yishuv* had to learn how to accept guidance from a woman. Szold's success is evident in her election in 1930 to serve on the Vaad Leumi, the National Council of Jews in Palestine, which entrusted her with the responsibility for social welfare. She trained social workers for the whole country and in 1941 initiated an educational and correctional system for young offenders.

At age seventy-three Szold wanted to return to America "to be coddled by my sisters," but her deep sense of responsibility made her shoulder a new undertaking. In 1933, Nazism had come to power in Germany, and German Jews began migrating to Palestine. The previous year had seen an increase in youth immigration into the area. Inevitably, Szold assumed the task of developing the Youth Aliyah movement initiated by Recha Freier. As organizer and leader of Youth

Hadassah-Hebrew University Medical Center, Jerusalem

Youth Aliyah activities included farming on kibbutzim.

Aliyah, Szold first established a program of education that would give individual attention to each child. Afterwards, she guided the immigration, reeducation, and resettlement of these children, striving to make personal contact with each child.

In 1942, Szold's concern for Arab-Jewish relations led her to join the Ihud (Unity) movement, an organization which promoted good relations between Arabs and Jews and supported the formation of a binational Arab-Jewish state in Palestine.

Henrietta Szold received many honors from Jews and non-Jews alike. But her enduring memorials are Hadassah, one of the most vigorous and important organizations of American Jewish women to this day, and her work on behalf of Youth Aliyah, which rescued thousands of Jewish children from the Nazi Holocaust, many of whom have become leaders in nearly every field in the reborn State of Israel. Szold continues to serve as a source of inspiration to young Jewish women in America, in Israel, and throughout the world.

🌿 🌿 🌿

A slightly younger contemporary of Henrietta Szold was Lillian Wald, a leading figure in the history of American social work. The major beneficiary of this remarkable woman's life's work was American society at large.

Wald was born in Cincinnati in 1867 to affluent German-Jewish immigrants who belonged to a Reform temple but did not give their daughter any formal Jewish training. After the family moved to Rochester, New York, young Lillian, who had no need to work and was expected to get married and lead a leisurely life, decided to become a nurse. Her family agreed to enroll her at the Bellevue School of Nursing in New York City.

After graduating in 1891, Wald worked for a year at the New York Juvenile Asylum. The turning point in her life came in 1893, when she visited the poor neighborhoods of New

Lillian Wald

56

York's Lower East Side, inhabited by recent immigrants from Europe. Like Szold's first visit to Jerusalem, where she saw disease and suffering, Wald's visit to the East Side exposed her to the poverty and substandard health conditions affecting recent immigrants. The young Jewish woman from New York's upper class was to become the saving angel of the poor and the sick.

Wald approached rich New York Jews, including Solomon Loeb, and asked them to sponsor nurses for the Lower East Side. Mrs. Loeb and her son-in-law, New York financier and philanthropist Jacob Schiff, agreed to sponsor two nurses.

Wald set up a nursing center in the poorest neighborhood of Lower Manhattan and began to work with the local residents, learning about their lives and problems. She organized the first visiting nurses service in the world, which in time would grow into a national service in the United States.

Wald now became a health reformer. When she discovered that the New York public school system did not have any school doctors, she took a boy suffering from scarlet fever out of a classroom and brought him to the city's health department. As a result, school doctors were dispatched to all the schools in New York.

As Wald's social work and nursing activities grew rapidly, she needed more space to work. She turned to her supporter, Jacob Schiff, for help. Schiff bought a house at 265 Henry Street for Wald and her staff. It became known as the Henry Street Settlement House. Its back yard became a playground for children and served as a model for city playgrounds throughout the United States. From the start, the settlement house was open to everyone, regardless of race or religion.

Although many Jewish immigrants benefitted from Wald's work, she did not think of herself primarily as a Jew. Her goal was to improve the lot of all people and see all immigrants become integrated in American society. The services of her settlement house expanded to include nursing, club work, and dramatic work, which were supplemented with vocational training for boys and girls, library services, and a savings bank. In the early 1900s,

Over broken asphalt, over dirty mattresses and heaps of refuse we went . . . There were two rooms and a family of seven not only lived here but shared their quarters with boarders . . . [I felt] ashamed of being a part of a society that permitted such conditions to exist . . . What I had seen had shown me where my path lay.
—Lillian Wald

Lower East Side, New York (early twentieth century)

the Settlement also opened branches in and around Manhattan and the Bronx, some specifically designed to serve the Italian, Hungarian, and African-American communities. By 1903, eighteen district nursing service centers treated 4,500 patients a year. Sick women, children, and workers were sent to Settlement "convalescent" homes on the Hudson River, and children took summer field trips to a Settlement-owned farm in Westchester County.

Lillian Wald commemorative medal

In 1915, Wald published the history of the Henry Street Settlement House and dedicated the book, titled *The House on Henry Street,* to "the comrades who have built the house." The book became a classic for generations of nursing, sociology, and social welfare students. The Settlement's activities continued to grow. In 1915 alone, one hundred nurses cared for more than 26,000 patients and made more than 227,000 home visits.

Wald was a firm believer in the women's suffrage movement and was even asked by the leaders of the movement to run for political office. Although she declined, Wald supported the New York State suffrage campaigns. When the 1915 amendment failed to pass, one suffrage leader blamed immigrant voters. Wald pointed out that many immigrants, and especially Jews, female and male, were anxious to exercise the political rights that they had been denied elsewhere. Wald, as always, saw the women of the Henry Street neighborhood as her primary constituents and continued to champion both the cause of suffrage and immigrant rights with equal zeal. She considered the successful campaign of 1917 a great victory.

In April 1917, with the U.S. at war in Europe, Wald, a pacifist, served as president of the American Union against Militarism. She found that support for her Visiting Nurse Service was declining. Despite her political beliefs, however, she helped the war effort, and at her recommendation, one of her nurses was made director of the U.S. Army School for Nursing.

In the 1920s Wald continued to work to improve health services and child welfare and increase peace and gender equality both nationally and internationally. During the Great Depression in the early 1930s, the Henry Street Settlement House became a major source of food for the hungry. On Wald's seventieth birthday, the radio aired a message read by President Roosevelt's mother in which the president praised Wald for her "unselfish labor to promote the happiness and well-being of others."

Wald died in 1940 at the age of seventy-three. She was mourned at many public gatherings, including 2,500 people at Carnegie Hall who heard messages from the president, governor, mayor, and others, testifying to her ability to bring people together and effect change. Henry Street House and the Visiting Nurse Service of New York continue the work initiated by Wald more than one hundred years ago. At its centennial in 1993, the Settlement highlighted its services, namely, addressing the needs of its contemporary neighbors through advocacy for the homeless, building AIDS awareness, combating illiteracy, fighting domestic violence, and offering programs for youths and seniors.

❧ ❧ ❧

The early years of the twentieth century in the United States were marked by social and economic upheaval. At the heart of the unrest was the workers' struggle for fair wages and decent working conditions. Millions of recent immigrants were employed in factories and worked under substandard conditions, without the protection of strong labor legislation, and at the mercy of the owners of big companies and industries who were largely apathetic to the welfare of their employees. Labor strikes were common and were often broken up violently, resulting in wounded and dead strikers.

In 1885, a sixteen-year-old Jewish woman named Emma Goldman arrived in the United States. Small in stature yet thundering like a prophet, she would become known as "Red Emma," a leading advocate of anarchism, a theory which maintains that all forms of government interfere unjustly with individual liberty and should be replaced by the voluntary association of cooperative groups.

While Henrietta Szold's Zionism resulted in the Jews' regaining their historical land, and Lillian Wald's social activism resulted in a more humane and just society in the United States, Emma Goldman's anarchism did not seem to lead anywhere, except to trouble. As a political philosophy, anarchism died like many other "isms" in the first half of the twentieth century. This has led some to conclude that Goldman lived the misguided and wasted life of a radical political leader who just happened to be born Jewish.

This, however, is too facile a conclusion. Goldman should be judged against the times in which she lived. When she left her native Lithuania in 1885 as a teenager and arrived in Roch-

The free expression of the hopes and aspirations of a people is the greatest and only safety in a sane society.
—Emma Goldman

59

ester, New York (where Lillian Wald, who was two years older, lived), she had to work in a corset factory where she earned $2.50 an hour. Working conditions were appalling. Young women were at the mercy of their employers. Health services were almost nonexistent, and many workers got sick and died young.

When she turned twenty, Goldman moved to New York and began to organize young women into labor unions. She was convinced that all forms of government—capitalist, communist, or any other—oppressed people. The best government was no government at all. Highly idealistic and a firm believer in the goodness in people, Goldman fought until the day she died for people to be able to run their affairs in total freedom, without any form of authority.

Like Wald, Goldman was a pacifist, opposed to the draft and to U.S. participation in World War I. During the war, she was sentenced to two years in jail for opposing the draft. In prison, she used her training as a nurse to help other female inmates.

In 1919, after the war had ended, Goldman was deemed "undesirable" and deported back to Europe. Considered pro-Communist, she was given the nickname "Red Emma." Her experience in the new Soviet Union, however, was far from happy. She found the Soviet system oppressive and was horrified by the hunger and suffering she saw everywhere. As far as she was concerned, Communism was no better than Capitalism. She wrote two books about her disillusionment with Russia, making herself unpopular on both sides of the ocean.

Goldman's last political involvement was her support of the anarchists in the Spanish Civil War in the late 1930s. She died in 1940 while traveling in Canada.

Looking back today at Goldman's life's work, we discover how much of what she taught and did has become incorporated into American life. She was one of the first proponents in America for women's rights, including full equality in the workplace and birth control. She was a vigorous champion of individual freedom. She advocated workers' right to organize and promoted the eight-hour work day, which was not the norm at that time. Like many political radicals of Jewish origin, Goldman did not embrace the teachings of Judaism. But her deep sense of justice was certainly rooted in her Jewish heritage.

Chapter Eight

Women During the Holocaust

The early years of the twentieth century produced three highly idealistic Jewish women who pursued a world free of oppression, inequality, and war. But when Henrietta Szold, Lillian Wald, and Emma Goldman died during the 1940s, the world plunged into World War II, the most devastating war in human history, during which one-third of the Jewish people was destroyed in what has become known as the Holocaust.

Jewish women living in Europe under the German occupation during World War II were in constant danger. In recent years, tens of thousands of oral and written testimonies of

Transport of women and children arriving at Auschwitz

Jewish women survivors of the Holocaust have been collected and published. Many of these women performed heroic acts during those years of horror by physically resisting the Nazis, risking their lives to save others, and setting an example of spiritual strength and courage in the face of ultimate evil.

When the war ended in 1945, the names of three women emerged from the ashes. Their nobility of character and great courage made them into present-day legends. Two—Hannah Szenes and Anne Frank—perished in the catastrophe. The third, Zivia Lubetkin, survived under the most impossible conditions to start a new life in the reborn State of Israel.

When the war broke out in 1939, Anne Frank was only ten. Hannah Szenes was eighteen. Zivia Lubetkin was twenty-five. All three dreamed of a better world for their people and for all people. All three were caught up in the war and came face to face with the Nazi beast. All three have left a legacy that has inspired and enriched people's lives to this day.

Zivia Lubetkin

❦ ❦ ❦

While attending high school in her native Poland before the war, Zivia Lubetkin became a devout Zionist. She was keenly aware of growing antisemitism in Poland, where Jews were barred from good jobs and treated as second-class citizens. She was determined to settle in the Land of Israel and help build the new Jewish state.

In her early twenties, Lubetkin became one of the leaders of Dror, a Zionist youth movement in Poland. She helped organize groups of young men and women who received vocational and agricultural training in Poland before moving to Palestine, where most of them started new settlements known as *kibbutzim*. She married a young Zionist leader named Yitzhak Zuckerman.

In the summer of 1939, on the eve of the German invasion of Poland which sparked World War II, Lubetkin was attending a Zionist congress in Switzerland. She faced the choice of either leaving for Palestine or risking her life by returning to Poland to help her people through a time of mortal danger. She chose to return to Poland. Under German occupation, all Zionist activities in Poland became illegal, and Lubetkin and her friends had to go underground. Lubetkin became one of the leaders of the Zionist underground. When traveling to keep in touch with groups of young Zionists, she often assumed the identity of a Polish gentile and constantly risked being found out by the Germans and executed on the spot.

During the war, Poland's Jewish population was concentrated in Warsaw, Poland's capital. There the Germans herded hundreds of thousands of Jews into a section of the city surrounded by a high wall and guarded day and night by heavily armed S.S. guards and watch dogs. People died in the ghetto every day from starvation, disease, and summary executions.

When the Germans began mass deportations of Jews from the Warsaw Ghetto to the death camp at Treblinka in central Poland, Zionist youth organizations in the ghetto began to organize Jewish resistance. Lubetkin was the only woman on the high command of the Jewish Fighting Organization, the ZOB, headed by Mordecai Anielewitz.

In the spring of 1943 it became clear that no Jew in the Warsaw Ghetto had any chance of surviving. Anielewitz and his high command decided to start an uprising against the Germans. They knew they could not win the battle against the Nazi war machine and had little chance of surviving. But they chose to die fighting rather than be sent like sheep to the slaughter at Treblinka.

Lubetkin and her husband fought in the uprising, against which the Germans sent special army units. The young Jewish fighters held out for weeks until finally, on May 8, 1943, the main bunker housing their high command fell, and Anielewitz, the leader of the uprising, was killed.

Lubetkin and her husband managed to escape. In August of that year they sent a telegram to the Polish government in exile, headquartered in London, informing it of the uprising and alerting the Jews of Western Europe to the fate awaiting them in the Nazi death camps in Poland. In October, Lubetkin joined the Polish revolt against the Germans. Although the Poles had not been supportive of the Jewish underground, Lubetkin decided to cooperate with them to fight the common enemy.

By the time Lubetkin and her husband left Poland in 1944, they had survived five years of constant danger to their lives. Together with other survivors of the ghetto's fighting groups they started a kibbutz in northern Israel called Lohamei Hagetaot, or "Ghetto Fighters." When Israel was born in 1948 and had to face the invading armies of seven Arab countries, Lubetkin and her friends served as a source of inspiration to

In any case, they had nothing to defend themselves with . . . It was then that we made our decision. We must resist! The question that we immediately asked ourselves was, "How, and with what?"
—Zivia Lubetkin

Zivia Lubetkin and Yitzhak Zuckerman

63

all young Israelis who vowed that never again would Jews be led like sheep to the slaughter.

❧ ❧ ❧

In 1944, the year Zivia Lubetkin and her husband arrived in Palestine, a twenty-two-year-old woman who lived on kibbutz Sdot Yam parachuted over Nazi-occupied Yugoslavia. Her mission was to make contact with Jewish leaders in her native Hungary and help organize Jewish resistance against the Nazis.

Hannah Szenes

Zionism did not come as naturally to Hannah Szenes (pronounced *Senesh*) as it did to Zivia Lubetkin. Her father, Bela Szenes, who died when she was six, was a well known Hungarian journalist and playwright. Her family had little interest in Judaism. At ten, Hannah was enrolled by her mother in a Protestant girls' high school. She received good grades, and at thirteen she began to keep a diary which she continued for the next ten years.

The virus of antisemitism that infected Europe did not spare Hungary. Young Hannah became preoccupied with the discrimination against the Jews of Hungary, as can be seen in her diary entries of that time, and she started to take an interest in Zionism. In 1938 she graduated from high school at the top of her class. She was eligible to start university studies, and she even entertained the thought of converting to Christianity. But by then it had become clear to her that her people needed her, and the best way to serve them was to become a pioneer in Palestine. She enrolled in the agricultural school in Nahalal, and two years later joined kibbutz Sdot Yam.

Having mastered modern Hebrew, she began to write poetry in her people's reborn language. One poem, "Eli Eli," has become a folk song and a modern prayer:

> *O Lord, my God,*
> *I pray that these things never end.*
> *The sand and the sea,*
> *The rush of the water,*
> *The crash of the heavens,*
> *The prayer of woman and man.*

World War II broke out in Europe while Szenes was living in Palestine. She was deeply concerned with the fate of her mother in Budapest and with that of Europe's Jews in general. At the time, many young Jews in Palestine enlisted in the British Army and formed the Jewish Brigade. Szenes, who had

64

joined the Haganah, or Jewish Defense Force, also enlisted. She became part of a select group of paratroopers who were dropped behind enemy lines in Europe to free allied prisoners of war, make contact with the Jewish communities in Europe, and organize Jewish resistance. Szenes was dropped in Yugoslavia. With the help of Yugoslav partisans, she crossed the border into Hungary, determined to find her mother and bring her to Palestine.

Szenes was soon captured by the Germans, thrown in jail, and subjected to a lengthy interrogation and severe torture. She stood up to her tormentors, refusing to divulge any information. Survivors of that jail attest to the courage and dignity of this unusual twenty-two-year-old woman. She was sentenced to death, and while awaiting execution wrote poetry. One of those poems has been sung in Israel for many years:

> *Blessed is the match that burned and kindled flames,*
> *Blessed is the flame that set hearts on fire.*
> *Blessed are the hearts that knew how to die with honor,*
> *Blessed is the match that burned, and kindled flames.*

❦ ❦ ❦

I pray that these things
never end.
The sand and the sea,
The rush of the water . . .
—Hannah Szenes

65

Anne Frank on an Israeli stamp

Born in Frankfurt, Germany in 1929, Anne Frank wanted to be a writer. When she was four, Hitler came to power in Germany, and her father, Otto Frank, realized that Jewish life in Germany was doomed. He moved the family to Amsterdam, where Anne was educated in a Dutch public school.

Anne was a keen observer of people and events during the darkest hour of Jewish history, showing a maturity beyond her years. When the Germans occupied Holland, Jews were not allowed to attend public schools, so Anne was transferred to a Jewish high school. She was outraged by how Jews were being treated by the occupiers. Still, she did not lose her serenity and optimism. She firmly believed that in the end justice would prevail, the Germans would be defeated, and Jews once again would be free and treated fairly.

In 1942, when Anne turned thirteen, the Germans began deporting Jews from Holland to concentration camps in Poland. No longer safe in their home, the Frank family went into hiding in a secret annex behind Otto Frank's office. There they remained for two years. During this time, Anne kept a diary to record her many observations of the people and events around her. She also wrote several short stories and began a novel.

At one point the Franks were denounced to the Germans. They were found, separated, and sent to two different concentrations camps. Anne and her older sister Margot were sent to Bergen Belsen in Germany, one of the most notorious death camps. It was December 1944, and the Liberation was only a few months away. But Anne fell ill and died in March 1945, as the war was about to end.

Otto Frank survived the war and returned to Holland in 1945. He was given his daughter's diary by a Dutch neighbor who had kept it. After several failed attempts, the diary was finally published in 1947. Almost immediately, Anne Frank became the voice of one and a half million Jewish children brutalized and murdered during the Holocaust. The book was translated into all major languages, published in countless editions, and made into a play and a motion picture. The portrait of the young teenager who appeared on the cover has become known to nearly every literate person on the planet.

Anne's famous words, "But I still believe in the good in man," became a message of forgiveness by an innocent victim to a world that stood by while six million innocent Jews were murdered. To the Jewish people, Anne Frank has become an example of a gifted daughter of Israel who was never given a chance to fulfill her life's potential, and a reminder that Jews must be ever vigilant to ensure that what happened in Europe during World War II never happens again.

Section of monument to the Warsaw Ghetto Uprising by Nathan Rappaport (1947)

From Judy Chicago's *Holocaust Project*: detail, Panel 1, "Sewing Circle" from "Double Jeopardy"

Kibbutz Family, by Johanan Simon

Chapter Nine

Women in the State of Israel

The new State of Israel was built by young idealistic men and women called *halutzim*, Hebrew for "pioneers." The first young pioneer women arrived in the Land of Israel in 1882. They belonged to a new Zionist group called BILU, an acronym derived from the biblical phrase, *Bet Yaacov, lechu venelacha*, "O house of Jacob, come, and let us go forth." They founded the first towns of what was to become present-day Israel, setting an example for several generations of young women who played a critical role in establishing the new state during the twentieth century.

Most of those women were well educated and came from fairly well-to-do families. They could have chosen academic careers and lived a comfortable life in Europe. But because they were strongly committed to the Zionist ideal of renewing Jewish life in the Land of Israel, they preferred to become common laborers and farmers and make that inhospitable ancient land flourish once again.

Not everyone was suited for this kind of life. Often romanticized as the life of suntanned, brawny young men and women who farmed the land by day and danced the *hora* around the campfire by night, it was a harsh and demand-

Leah Hervet, a BILU member who founded Gedera, with her grand-daughter

Courtesy of the Zionist Archives and Library, New York

69

ing existence that taxed the soul and required great endurance. But the twenty BILU pioneers who arrived in 1882 persevered, and by the time the State of Israel was born in 1947, its population had grown to half a million. Fifty years later, by the end of the twentieth century, Israel was a nation of five million. The Zionist dream had become a reality.

The young pioneers who built the state established an egalitarian society. Most of the young women who left Europe had mothers who had stayed at home to rear large families. The younger women, in sharp contrast, worked on farms and in factories alongside the men, and had only one or two children each. They participated in paramilitary activities, dressed simply, often wearing pants and rarely wearing makeup, and sought to prove they could do nearly anything men could, and certain things even better.

Still, they did not enjoy total equality. European immigrants brought their prejudices against women to the Promised Land, and Sephardic Jews from the Arab world brought theirs. Still today, women in Israel are struggling for full equality, both in the general Jewish community and in the smaller Orthodox community. In this chapter, we will meet some of the women who made unique contributions to the formation of the State of Israel, and some of those who have taken the lead in recent years.

❦   ❦   ❦

Sarah Aaronsohn and her brother Aaron (top), with another brother and Sarah's husband

When Sarah Aaronsohn was born in Palestine in 1890, there were very few Jewish farming families in the Promised Land. The Aaronsohn family of Zichron Yaakov was one of the first. Sarah's father was a skillful farmer, and the family prospered and became one of the most prominent in the country. One son, Aaron, became the country's leading agronomist. Among his accomplishments was the discovery of wild wheat in the Galilee. Sarah, fourteen years Aaron's junior, was close to her brother.

World War I began when Sarah was twenty-four. At that time Palestine was ruled by the Turks, who opposed Jewish settlement. In fact, the Turkish Empire was about to collapse, and the Turks showed extreme cruelty in fighting their opponents. In the Turkish region of Anatolia, they massacred millions of Christian Armenians. At that time newly married, Sarah lived in Turkey and traveled to Anatolia. The atrocities she saw committed against the Armenians there made her deeply concerned with the fate of her own people in Palestine.

Back home in Zichron Yaakov, she communicated her concern to her brother Aaron, who was then working with the Turkish administration in Palestine and was appalled at the way the Turkish rulers were treating the Jewish pioneers. Greatly moved by his sister's account, he decided the only hope was to overthrow Turkish rule.

To accomplish this, Aaron, Sarah, and their brother Alexander organized an intelligence-gathering group called NILI, an acronym for the Hebrew phrase *netzah Yisrael lo yeshaker,* or "the Eternal Rock of Israel will not fail." The purpose of the group was to make contact with the British, who were preparing to invade Palestine and end Turkish rule, and provide them with firsthand accounts of Turkish troop movement and other strategic information.

Aaron Aaronsohn made contact with British intelligence, who approved of his plans. Sarah soon became a vital link in gathering intelligence from the NILI agents and providing it to the British. The information NILI supplied to the British proved vital to the war effort and greatly advanced the British campaign in Palestine.

Leaders of the Jewish community in Palestine did not support NILI's activities. The idea of Jews involved in espionage was foreign to them, and they were afraid of what the Turks might do if they found out. During the war, the Turks forced the Jews of Jaffa and Tel Aviv to evacuate their homes and banished them to the North as a punitive measure. Aware of what the Turks had done to the Armenians, Jewish leaders feared the worst. NILI had to operate under extremely precarious conditions.

Sarah Aaronsohn traveled to Egypt to make contact with the British military high command. While in Cairo, she found out that the Turks had discovered the existence of NILI. Her associates counseled her to remain in Cairo, since it was unsafe for her to return home. However, concerned with the fate of her colleagues in Palestine, she decided to go back and help them. She returned to Zichron Yaakov and ordered her colleagues to disperse, so as not to be caught by the Turks. In order not to arouse suspicion, she herself returned home and pretended to lead an ordinary life on her family's farm.

The Turkish secret police went to Sarah's home and arrested her. For four days she was subjected to a series of interrogations during which she was tied to a post, whipped, and beaten. She would not divulge any names. She was then told

Sarah Aaronsohn on a recent stamp

The Eternal Rock of Israel will not fail.
—Sarah and Aaron Aaronsohn, quoting the Bible

71

she would be sent to Nazareth, to the regional Turkish head-quarters for northern Palestine, where the Turks had more sophisticated torture methods which would prove more effective in making her talk.

Aaronsohn asked her tormentors to let her go home and change her soiled and bloody clothes, since it would make a very bad impression if she were taken to Nazareth looking the way she did. They agreed. She went into her bathroom, took out a pistol, and shot herself in the head. She was twenty-seven years old.

Two years later, Aaron Aaronsohn's plane would mysteriously disappear over the British Channel on the way to a peace conference in France.

Today, Israel has one of the best intelligence services in the world, the Mosad, which has played a critical role in protecting and preserving the young state. It all began with the sacrifice of a brave woman named Sarah Aaronsohn.

In 1890, the year Sarah Aaronsohn was born, another woman who would help define the character of Israeli society was born in Saratov, on the Volga River in northern Russia. Her name was Rachel Bluwstein. In Israel she is known simply as Ra'hel. While Aaronsohn's activities are an example of great courage and self-sacrifice, Ra'hel's poems became words to live by, helping form the new Hebrew language and culture, and shaping the dreams and yearnings of young Israelis as they pursued the difficult task of building the new state.

Growing up in Russia, Ra'hel started writing poems in Russian at age fifteen. She also studied painting. Unlike the vivacious, fearless Sarah Aaronsohn, Ra'hel was not made of the stuff heroes are made of. In fact, it is hard to understand what prompted her, at age nineteen, to leave her home and her Russian culture and go to Palestine, where she did not speak the language and where she became one of the first trainees at the young women's training farm at Kinneret, on the Sea of Galilee. About her life in those early days she wrote:

> How did we spend the day at Kinneret? We started working at dawn. We were fourteen young women with blistered hands, barefoot, suntanned, scratched, full of defiance, our hearts blazing. The air was full of our singing, chatting, laughter. The hoes went up and

Ra'hel

down, up and down, ceaselessly. You would stop for a second, wipe your brow with the edge of your *keffiyeh* [Arab headgear], and sneak a loving glance at the Sea of Galilee. It's so good! So blue, silent blue, peaceful blue, heartwarming blue. Somewhere a bird hovers over the blue, and soon the tiny steamboat shuttling between Zemach and Tiberias will start blowing smoke.

Ra'hel's romantic recollection of her early days in Palestine only thinly disguises the harsh reality facing a frail and dreamy young woman who undertook a task beyond her physical strength. But her boundless love for the land and her burning desire to make it bloom again helped her overlook many hardships.

Ra'hel quickly mastered the Hebrew language, which in those days was still largely the old formal language of the Bible, rather than the present-day idiom of everyday life in Israel. She began to write short poems in her newly acquired tongue, in which she captured the spirit of the young pioneers, creating a new Hebrew style that was simple, direct, soulful, and full of love for the land and honest work. The poems soon became popular. Several of them were set to music and sung over and over again like prayers which lifted the spirits of young men and women who were building the new land.

One of the beloved poems of those days and for many years thereafter was simply titled *Ve'ulai*, "Perhaps":

> *Perhaps it never happened*
> *Perhaps*
> *I never rose at dawn*
> *To till the soil with the sweat of my*
> *brow.*
>
> *Did I ever, on long sweltering*
> *Harvest days*
> *From atop a wagon laden with sheaves*
> *Break into song?*
>
> *Did I ever cleanse myself in the calm blue,*
> *In the purity*
> *Of my Kinneret . . . oh, my Sea of Galilee,*
> *Was it you, or was it only a dream?*

Her blood runs in mine,
Her voice sings within me—
Rachel who tends Laban's flocks,
Rachel—mother's mother.
—Ra'hel

Sea of Galilee

73

In 1913, at age twenty-three, Ra'hel went to France to study agronomy. World War I broke out the following year and prevented her from returning to Palestine. Instead, she went back to Russia where she taught Jewish refugee children. When she returned to Palestine after the war she settled in Degania, a new *kibbutz,* or agricultural settlement, near the Sea of Galilee. Degania was first organized in 1909 by a group of young pioneers who agreed not to have any children until the new venture became well established. The first couple to break the agreement was the Dayans. They gave birth to a child whom they named Moshe. He would become Israel's most illustrious military hero. In later years Moshe Dayan would recall how Ra'hel took care of him when he was five. He never forgot her pale and noble face. Her poetry had a great impact on his life both as a child and as an adult.

But Ra'hel was not able to take care of children in the kibbutz for long. During the war she had contracted tuberculosis, and soon after arriving at Degania she became too ill for farm life. She spent the rest of her days in hospitals and sanatoria.

Bedridden, she continued to write poetry. Some of those later poems express her regret at not being able to be of greater service to her land. One of those poems is titled "To My Land."

I never sang for you, my land
I didn't glorify your name
With mighty deeds
Or bravery in battle.
A little sapling my hands did plant
On silent Jordan's bank,
A little path my feet made
Across the fields.
Indeed, how poor my offering,
I know, dear mother,
Indeed, how poor
Your daughter's gift.
Only a shout of joy
The day the light would shine,
Only hidden tears
For your misery.

In 1931, at age forty-one, Ra'hel succumbed to her illness. She did not live long enough to see "the day the light would shine," namely, the day Israel was born in 1948. But to this day children and adults in Israel sing her songs, memorize her poems, and speak an everyday language she helped shape.

There is hardly a literate person on this planet who has not heard of a woman named Golda Meir. She is known as one of the builders and leaders of the State of Israel. But this is only half the story. The other half is Golda Meir the woman, known to Israelis as "Our Golda" and to the rest of the world as one of the greatest women of the twentieth century, perhaps of all time.

Simple-mannered and plain-speaking, Meir would be the first to dismiss such praise. Many remember her as a typical Jewish grandmother, except for the fact that she was a chain-smoker. When she showed up at a public forum to make a speech—whether in Israel, at the United Nations, or anywhere around the world—one would wonder at first whether she was a cleaning woman who had approached the podium by mistake. But once Meir started to speak everyone listened. The plain-looking woman who spoke simple words held everyone in rapt attention. Even those who disagreed with her found truth in her words.

Golda Mabovitch was born in 1898 in Russia where, as a little girl, she had firsthand experience of pogroms, or attacks on Jews by local peasants. When she was eight, her family immigrated to the U.S. and settled in Milwaukee, where she graduated from high school and enrolled in a teachers' college. At seventeen she became an active Zionist, and soon she decided that to her Zionism meant settling in Palestine and becoming a pioneer.

In 1921 she persuaded her husband, Morris Myerson, to accompany her to Palestine and join a kibbutz. She quickly adapted to the hard life on kibbutz Merhavia in the malaria-ridden valley south of Nazareth, but after a few years her talents as a speaker and an organizer made her one of the leaders of the labor movement. In 1928 she became the executive secretary of the movement's Women's Labor Council.

In those years most men and women in Palestine belonged to a labor union called the Histadrut. It was the most powerful organization of the pre-state years. In 1934 Golda Meir became the head of the Political Department of the Histadrut. This provided her with the training necessary for her future political role in the new state.

Courtesy of *The Washington Jewish Week*

Golda, age eight, arrives in the United States

75

In August 1939, Golda Meir attended the Zionist Congress in Switzerland. There she met a young woman from Poland named Zivia Lubetkin, who later became a leader in the Warsaw Ghetto Uprising. A month later, the Nazis would invade Poland and the Holocaust would start. Lubetkin would choose to go back to Poland and help her people there. Meir would go back to Palestine to continue her political work of building the new state.

In her book *My Life*, Meir writes:

Courtesy of *The Washington Jewish Week*

Golda Meir, Prime Minister of Israel

I have often replayed in my mind those relatively optimistic conversations we had in my room in Geneva toward the end of August, 1939. All but a few of those dedicated young people perished later in Auschwitz, Maidanek, and Sobibor. But among them were the leaders of the Jewish resistance movements of Eastern Europe who fought the Nazis inside the ghettos, outside them with the partisans, and finally behind the electrified barbed wire of the death camps. I can hardly bear to think of them now, but I believe with all my heart that one of the things that made it possible for them to go on fighting against such odds to the very end was the knowledge that we were with them all the time and so they were never really alone. I am not particularly given to mysticism, but I hope I will be pardoned for saying that in our darkest hours it was the memory of their spirit that gave us heart, inspiring us to go on and, above all, lent validity to our refusal to be wiped out to make life easier for the rest of the world. In the final analysis, it was the Jews of Europe, trapped, doomed, and destroyed, who taught us once and for all that we must become the masters of our own undertaking, and I think it can be said that we have kept faith with them (p. 165).

The State of Israel was born out of the ashes of the Holocaust. Would there have been an Israel without the Holocaust? Perhaps. But the Holocaust, as Meir points out, completely transformed people like her and the rest of the Jewish world.

When World War II ended, the leaders of the *yishuv* (Jewish community) renewed their struggle against British rule in Palestine. The urgency of proclaiming the new state in the aftermath of the Holocaust became paramount. In June 1946 the British arrested all the top leaders of the *yishuv*. Although

Meir was in the forefront of the struggle, she was not arrested and became the main representative of the Jewish population before the British. She served as head of the Political Department of the Jewish Agency, the leading body of the *yishuv*, until the establishment of the State of Israel in 1948.

In January 1948 Golda Meir went to the United States on a critical mission. The embryonic state was financially broke. There was no money to absorb immigrants, buy food, or obtain arms necessary for the impending conflict with the Arab states who promised to "push the Jews into the sea." The last hope was American Jewry. At the time, U.S. Secretary of State George C. Marshall advised the leader of the *yishuv*, David Ben-Gurion, to defer the proclamation of the state, since Marshall did not believe a tiny Jewish state could defeat seven Arab armies.

Meir met with a large gathering of American Jewish leaders in Chicago. She told them she had not come to ask for advice whether or not to proclaim the state, or whether or not to engage in an armed conflict. This was for the Jews in Palestine to decide. She came because in order to win, her people needed financial support from their American brothers and sisters. Her message hit the mark. She raised the unheard of sum of fifty million dollars, without which Israel would barely have survived the first critical months of its existence.

Upon Meir's return to Israel, she was sent on another historic mission. This time she risked her life by traveling into enemy territory to meet with King Abdullah of Jordan. Disguised as an Arab, she met with the king and tried to persuade him not to join the Arab opposition to the new state. The king was sympathetic but made it clear he could not go against the wishes of his Arab allies. Still, the meeting paved the way for future relations between Israel and Jordan, ultimately leading to a peace treaty between the two countries.

After the birth of the state, Meir was given the delicate task of serving as Israel's first emissary to Moscow. At the time, over three million Jews were living in the Soviet Union. Stalin's reign of terror had reached its peak, and among his main victims were the Jews. Most synagogues and Hebrew schools had been eliminated. Even the Yiddish writers and actors who were loyal to the Communist regime had been jailed, and some were executed on trumped-up charges. When Golda Meir arrived in Moscow in September 1948, thousands of Jews who had been afraid to be openly identified as Jews defied the regime and gathered in the streets around Moscow's one official synagogue, where Israel's newly appointed emissary attended Rosh Hashanah services. In *My Life,* Meir writes about the experience:

> They had come—those good, brave Jews—in order to be with us, to demonstrate their sense of kinship and to celebrate the establishment of the State of Israel. Within seconds they had surrounded me, almost lifting me bodily, almost crushing me, saying my name over and over again . . . Without speeches or parades, without any words at all really, the Jews of Moscow were proving their profound desire—and their need— to participate in the miracle of the establishment of the Jewish state, and I was the symbol of the state for them (p. 250).

Back in Israel the following year, Meir was appointed minister of labor, becoming the only woman in Ben-Gurion's government. Over a million new immigrants had arrived in the new state, and large-scale housing and road projects were underway. Meir supervised this undertaking and refused to restrict immigration, no matter the cost. A master of the impos-

Jews crowd around Ms. Meir as she leaves the Moscow synagogue while serving as Israel's first minister to the Soviet Union

Courtesy of *The Washington Jewish Week*

sible, she continued to perform one miracle after another.

In 1956 Meir became foreign minister, a post she held until 1965. During those years Israel was politically isolated, with the Arab League imposing an economic boycott on the new state and with many countries preferring Arab oil to friendship with the struggling new state. Meir did not have an easy task addressing the United Nations or making friends for Israel around the world. But everywhere she went, she commanded the respect of her listeners, no matter how opposed they were to her message. Among her achievements during those years was the aid she extended to some of the new African states, where Israelis taught the local people farming methods and health care, and provided other vital services.

In 1969 Meir became Israel's fourth prime minister. By this time, she had become ill with cancer but kept it a secret so she could continue to hold high public office. It was a time of euphoria for Israel. Two years earlier, in 1967, Israel had won a stunning military victory against the Arabs in the Six Day War. Meir offered to make peace with the Arab neighbors but was turned down. The Arabs were secretly preparing for the next war, which caught Israel unprepared on Yom Kippur of 1973. Thousands of Israeli soldiers were wounded and killed during the first days of the war. Even though Israel was victorious in the end, Meir never recovered from the experience. As prime minister, she took responsibility for the initial fiasco, and rumor has it she even contemplated suicide. She resigned from government and was replaced by Yitzhak Rabin. Four years later, she passed away.

Meir remains one of the Jewish people's most admired and beloved figures of the twentieth century. After the Yom Kippur War, she said that in time the Israelis might forgive the Arabs "for killing our sons," but "it would be much harder to forgive them for forcing us to kill their sons." When someone told her the Jews were smart people, she replied, "How can we be smart when we picked the only country in the Middle East that does not have oil?"

The pioneering efforts of Sarah Aaronsohn, Ra'hel, and Golda Meir made the State of Israel possible. The role of women in Israel has been growing and expanding over the years. Today, women are playing a central role in Israel's politics, law, business, literature, sports, and more. Below are a few examples of such women.

❧   ❧   ❧

We must become the masters of our own undertakings.
—Golda Meir

79

Geulah Cohen as a young underground fighter

My friends, who also
dreamed by day,
When others were wide
awake.
Who also fought at night,
When others slept.
—Geulah Cohen

Two controversial women who have left their mark on Israeli politics in past decades are Geulah Cohen and Shulamit Aloni. The first represents the extreme right of the Zionist political spectrum, and the second the extreme left. Both made many enemies, were often denounced, and were attacked verbally and physically. Both eventually retired from politics because of their radical views. Yet both made unique contributions because they were not willing to leave well enough alone and were not afraid to put themselves at risk to bring about change.

Geulah Cohen was a teenager in the 1940s, during the years of struggle for the establishment of Israel. Articulate and fearless, she joined the most extreme underground group fighting British rule, the Stern Group, known officially as LEHI (Fighters for the Freedom of Israel). The members of LEHI were constantly hunted by British secret police and were considered extremely dangerous. Cohen became LEHI's radio announcer. In her illegal broadcasts she reported the group's exploits and denounced British rule. Twice she was captured and jailed, and twice she escaped from heavily guarded prisons. The second time she remained free until the birth of the state.

After the founding of the state, Geulah Cohen became active in Israeli politics. She was elected to the Knesset, or Israeli parliament, and continued to speak up where others sought compromise. A gifted writer and speaker, she was one of the first in the late 1960s to speak up and write about the plight of Soviet Jewry. Thanks to activists like her in Israel and around the world, in 1970 the Soviet Union for the first time allowed some Jews to leave the country, starting what became a mass exodus of Jews seeking freedom.

When President Jimmy Carter went to Israel to address the Knesset during the peace talks between Israel and Egypt, Knesset Member Geulah Cohen made headlines around the world when she heckled the American president. In so doing, she broke ranks with Prime Minister Menachem Begin, with whom she had identified politically. Later she opposed her former LEHI commander, Prime Minister Yitzhak Shamir, when he began negotiations with the Palestinians in Madrid.

Cohen remains opposed to returning one inch of the Land of Israel to the Arabs. In recent years her son, Tzachi Hanegbi, became justice minister in Prime Minister Binyamin Netanyahu's government. Himself a right-wing politician, Hanegbi's highly sensitive office has forced him to moderate his views. True to form, his mother, while admitting she understood him, refused to approve of his actions. Geulah Cohen remains the voice of uncompromising Israeli nationalism.

❦   ❦   ❦

Shulamit Aloni was also a teenager in 1948, when Israel was born. Like Geulah Cohen, Aloni's voice was heard in public forums, reported in print, and carried on the radio. Both women seemed to thrive on controversy. But while Cohen belonged to the outlawed far right, Aloni was a member of the so-called "establishment"—the Israeli ruling labor party of David Ben-Gurion and Golda Meir.

In Israel's 1948 War of Independence, Aloni was a soldier in the Palmach, the elite units of the Israel Defense Force, and fought on the most difficult front—the Old City of Jerusalem. She was taken prisoner by the Jordanian Army.

In the new state she became a teacher and one of the first Israeli civil rights activists. Like Cohen, she became a Member of the Knesset (MK) in 1965 and remained an MK for nearly thirty years.

While Cohen was the gadfly of the right, Aloni became the gadfly of the left. Like Cohen, she felt compelled to speak out for Soviet Jewry in 1969, when the Israeli government was afraid to do so because of Soviet repercussions. Aloni was also critical of the religious parties for not allowing Israel's citizens freedom of choice in personal status matters, such as marriage and divorce. She even established the "Shulamit Aloni marriage," a civil ceremony which bypassed rabbinical authority. Labor leaders like Golda Meir disapproved of Aloni's actions, and in 1973 Aloni formed her own party, the Civil Rights Movement.

When dubbed a "women's libber," she rejected the title, arguing that she was committed to human rights for all, regardless of gender, religion, or nationality.

In 1992 Aloni combined three small parties in the Knesset, including her own, and campaigned under the banner of human rights. She won twelve seats in the election, making her new party, Meretz, the third largest. She joined Prime Minister Yitzhak Rabin's government as minister of education.

Aloni's actions over the next four years were extremely controversial. She spoke out on every imaginable issue related to human rights and social justice. While addressing a Jewish gathering in New York, she was physically attacked by Orthodox Jews who considered her an enemy of Judaism. In 1996, at odds with her own party's leadership, she retired from po-

I am for peoples' liberation, men and women. I am a "human libber."
—Shulamit Aloni

Shulamit Aloni

81

litical life.

The issues Shulamit Aloni fought for during her long years of public service are now some of the most burning issues facing Israeli society as the peace process with the Arabs progresses and domestic issues become more urgent. Some issues may take years to resolve. Aloni, however, will undoubtedly be remembered as one of the pioneers of civil rights in the new state.

Both Geulah Cohen and Shulamit Aloni will be remembered as courageous women who, although representing two extremes on Israel's political map, were deeply committed to the welfare of their people and fought in their own way for what they believed was right.

Two women who have greatly enriched Israeli culture over the years are Nehama Leibowitz and Dahlia Ravikovitch. The first was one of the greatest Torah teachers and scholars of the twentieth century. The second is Israel's leading woman poet. Leibowitz represents Israel's Orthodox, traditional culture. Ravikovitch is the voice of Israel's new, secular culture. Both have won many accolades for their accomplishments.

When Nehama Leibowitz died in 1997 at the age of ninety-two, she was mourned by thousands throughout the Jewish world. Her mission in life was to impart the knowledge of the Bible to as many people as possible in Israel and around the world, whether Orthodox or secular, rabbi or scientist, young or old.

Leibowitz herself came from an Orthodox family in Latvia. When she was little, her family moved to Berlin, where she later received a doctorate in biblical studies. A traditional, observant Jew, she was exposed to modern biblical scholarship and applied new methods of biblical research to the traditional Jewish commentaries. In 1931 she settled in Palestine, where over sixty years she taught three generations of teachers. Leibowitz's teaching and research methods revitalized the study of the Five Books of Moses and had a far-reaching impact on many teachers and rabbis throughout the world.

Pleased with the influence her work had on so many people, Leibowitz said:

I am enthralled by this vast army of old and young,

Nehama Leibowitz

mothers and girls, teachers male and female, clerks and laborers, veterans and newcomers of all communities, hundreds of thousands (literally!) studying Torah for its own sake. For our joint studies involved no certificates, examinations, marks, prizes; no credits, scholarships, income-tax rebates but simply the joy so deep of the one who studies Torah.

One of Leibowitz's great skills as a teacher was asking her students thought-provoking questions that deepened their understanding of the biblical text. Here is one of her questions regarding a Talmudic observation about the creation of woman from man's rib:

> "And the Almighty built the rib"—this shows us that the Holy One gave woman more understanding than man [note: this is a play on words, since "built" (*banah*) is the same word form in Hebrew as "understanding" (*binah*)]. On what linguistic and extra-linguistic grounds is this homiletical interpretation based? What quality did our Sages refer to in the phrase "more understanding" with which they credited woman more than man?

In 1957 Leibowitz received the Israel Prize, the highest honor in Israel, in recognition of her teaching. In 1982 she received the Bialik Prize in literature and Jewish studies.

A simple, unassuming woman who always wore a plain suit and a dark brown beret tilted to one side, she never used a formal title but was known to all as "Nehama." When Bar-Ilan University in Israel conferred on her an honorary doctorate, she refused to wear a cap and gown, and appeared in her usual brown dress and beret.

A great teacher of Torah, Nehama Leibowitz followed the tradition of the great rabbis of Israel. Many Orthodox Jews, especially women, believe she deserves the title "rabbi." Her teachings of the weekly Torah portion and her Bible commentaries continue to enrich the entire Jewish world.

❦   ❦   ❦

In 1998, on Israel's fiftieth anniversary, Dahlia Ravikovitch received the Israel Prize for literature for her poetic achievements. This shy and reclusive woman thus received official recognition as Israel's greatest living woman poet.

Ravikovitch's poetry is directly descended from the poetic

I am enthralled by this vast army of old and young . . . studying Torah for its own sake.
—Nehama Leibowitz

Daliah Ravikovitch

work of Miriam and Deborah in the Bible. In fact, the Bible is Ravikovitch's favorite book and the main influence on her poetry. Unlike Nehama Leibowitz, who approached the Bible as a book of faith and explored the traditional commentaries, Ravikovitch, a native-born Israeli, reads the Bible as the early history and poetry of her people and her land, and the primary source of her native language.

Ravikovitch was born in Ramat Gan in 1939. Her father died when she was six, the victim of a hit-and-run accident. The bereaved family joined a kibbutz. The loss left a lasting mark on her. Life on the collective farm also affected her, since she was more inclined toward being a private person. As a young teenager she began writing poetry to express her inner conflicts. She was influenced by other Hebrew poets, including Leah Goldberg and Ra'hel. In fact, it was Goldberg who discovered the young poet and helped her get published. Since 1962, when Ravikovitch's first volume of poetry was published, she has written hundreds of poems which have become popular with readers of all ages.

Ravikovitch's poetry is very personal, as can be seen in the untitled poem about the loss of her father. Combining classical and contemporary Hebrew in a new style, it has a haunting quality and reads almost like a secular Kaddish for the dead parent:

> Standing on the road at night is this man
> Who once was my father.
> And I must go and stand there
> Because I was his oldest daughter.
>
> Every single night he stands alone on that spot
> And I must go down there and be there.
> And I wanted to ask the man until when must I,
> But I already knew I must always.
>
> The spot where he stands is dangerous
> As on the day he walked on the road and was run over by
> a car.
> And this is how I recognized him and I identified him
> As the man himself who once was my father.
>
> But he does not speak one word of love to me
> Although once he was my father
> And although I am his oldest daughter
> He cannot speak one word of love to me.

Her poems are often full of a sense of loss, pain, and questioning. But they are also rich in beautiful imagery and a rhythm which lingers in the imagination. About the untimely death during World War II of the famous French writer Antoine de Saint-Exupéry, author of *The Little Prince,* she writes:

People don't live forever
Neither are we forever
But if he had survived
That time in March,
Nineteen forty-three
He would be with us
A sparkling grain of sand
A flower in the wind
Laughing in the clouds.

Great Israeli Performers

Shoshana Damari was Israel's most popular singer before and after the birth of the state. In later years she became a world-renowned painter of folk art.

Ofra Haza is one of Israel's favorite folk singers. She is also known for her newspaper editorials about Israeli society.

Chapter Ten

Women in Science and Medicine

Many Jewish women today in Israel, the U.S., and around the world are engaged in science and medicine. Many are involved in advanced research, and in the twenty-first century one or more of them may contribute to finding a cure for cancer or to some other major breakthrough that will greatly improve human life.

Not so long ago, however, things were much different. First, it was very difficult for women to pursue a scientific or medical career. Second, it was far harder for a Jew to be accepted to the top schools of science and medicine, and nearly impossible for a Jewish woman.

There were, however, a few pioneers in Europe and in the United States, and some even received international recognition in the form of the world's most coveted award, the Nobel Prize. We will take a look here at a European Jewish woman and an American Jewish woman, both of whom made major contributions to the world of science and medicine.

Albert Einstein, the greatest scientist of the twentieth century, said early in the century when he first conceived of the theory of relativity and waited for it to be validated, "If I am proven to be right, the Germans will say I am a German. The Swiss will say I am a Swiss [he was a German citizen living in Switzerland at the time]. Everyone will disregard the fact that I am a Jew. If I am wrong, the Germans will say I am a Swiss, and the Swiss will say I am a German, and everyone will say I am a Jew."

Cancer research at the Department of Microbiology, Tel Aviv University

Rita Levi-Montalcini

This is more or less what happened to one of the great women scientists of our time, Rita Levi-Montalcini. She was born in Turin, Italy in 1909, to Adamo Levi and Adele Montalcini, an assimilated Italian Jewish couple who gave their daughter no Jewish education and little formal education. When Rita turned twenty, someone close to her died of cancer, and she decided to dedicate her life to medical research. Much the same way a young Catholic woman decides to become a nun and be married to the Church rather than raise a family, Levi-Montalcini decided to devote her entire life to science, to the exclusion of everything else.

Reluctantly, her family agreed to have her enrolled in the Turin School of Medicine, where she met Giuseppe Levi, a celebrated professor of medicine who inspired her to pursue research in neurology. In 1936 Levi-Montalcini received her medical degree.

At that time Italy was under the Fascist rule of Mussolini, who later became an ally of Hitler. The Fascist government was antisemitic, and all Jews were removed from university posts and not allowed to practice medicine. Levi-Montalcini found herself without a job.

In 1939 she joined her mentor, Dr. Levi, in Belgium. There she resumed her lifelong neurological research. Soon, however, the Nazis invaded Belgium, and she was forced to return to her native Turin. Dr. Levi accompanied her and worked with her there. When she wrote a report on the results of her research it was rejected for publication by the Fascists because of her "belonging to the Jewish race." When it was instead published in Belgium, Levi-Montalcini's reputation was established.

When conditions turned dangerous, she and her family went into hiding in Florence from 1943 until the end of the war in 1945. In 1947 Levi-Montalcini accepted a post at Washington University in St. Louis, Missouri, with the zoologist Viktor Hamburger, who was studying the growth of nerve tissue in chick embryos. In 1948 it was discovered in Hamburger's laboratory that a variety of mouse tumor spurred nerve growth when implanted into chick embryos. Levi-Montalcini and Hamburger traced the effect to a substance in the tumor that they named "Nerve Growth Factor" (NGF). Levi-Montalcini showed that the tumor caused similar cell growth in a nerve-tissue culture kept alive in the laboratory. Another scientist, Stanley Cohen, who by then had joined her at Washington University, was able to isolate the nerve-growth factor from the tumor. NGF was the first of many cell-growth factors to be found in animals. It plays an important role in the growth of nerve cells and fibers in the peripheral nervous system.

In 1956 Levi-Montalcini became a U.S. citizen but retained her Italian citizenship. In 1961 she returned to Italy and opened a research laboratory in Rome.

In 1986 she and Stanley Cohen won the Albert Lasker Medical Research Award. A few weeks later, they were jointly awarded the Nobel Prize in medicine for discovering NGF, which according to the Nobel Prize committee "held out the prospect of shedding light on many disorders, such as cancers, the delayed healing of wounds, and senile dementia, including Alzheimer's disease."

In 1987 the United States awarded Levi-Montalcini the National Medal of Science, the highest science award in America. In 1998, at nearly ninety years old, Levi-Montalcini continued her study of the effect of NGF on nervous, endocrine, and immune systems. Hers has been a life of total dedication to the cause of science.

❧   ❧   ❧

American-born Rosalyn Sussman Yalow, twelve years younger than Levi-Montalcini, was exposed to a lesser degree of antisemitism than Levi-Montalcini. But when Yalow graduated from Hunter College in New York with honors in 1941 and was anxious to go to medical school, she realized that as a woman and a Jew she had little chance of being admitted. Instead, she decided to study physics. When she applied to Purdue University, the school responded as follows: "She is from New York. She is Jewish. She is a woman. If you can guarantee her a job afterwards, we'll give her an assistantship." No such job guarantee was available, so she enrolled in secretarial school.

Rosalyn Yalow

But Yalow's luck changed when the U.S. entered World War II. Graduate schools lost students and had to admit women or be forced to close their doors. Yalow was given a teaching assistantship in physics at the University of Illinois' College of Engineering. She was the only woman among the faculty of hundreds, and when she received her doctorate in nuclear physics she was only the second woman in the history of the school to receive a doctoral degree.

In 1943 she married Aaron Yalow, a fellow physics student and the son of a rabbi from upstate New York.

From 1946 to 1950 she taught physics at Hunter College in New York City, and in 1947 she became a consultant in nuclear physics at the Veterans Administration Hospital in the Bronx, where research was conducted on the medical applications of radioactive materials.

In 1950 she left Hunter College to become assistant head of radioisotope service at the VA hospital. She started working with Dr. Solomon Berson, using radioactive isotopes to investigate physiological systems. The two created a new analytic technique called radioimmunoassay, or RIA, to quantify minute amounts of biological substances in body fluids using radioactive-labeled material. They made it possible for doctors to diagnose conditions caused by slight changes in hormone levels.

In 1959 Berson and Yalow used RIA to show that adult diabetics did not always suffer an insufficiency of insulin in their blood and that some unknown factor must be blocking the action of insulin. They also showed that the injected insulin obtained from animals was being inactivated by the patients' immune system. RIA was then used by other investigators for such purposes as screening blood for hepatitis virus in blood ranks, determining effective dosage levels of drugs and antibiotics, detecting foreign substances in the blood, treating dwarfed children with growth hormones, and testing and correcting hormone levels in infertile couples. The discovery of RIA has been called one of the most significant applications of basic research to clinical medicine.

Since the 1960s, Yalow has received dozens of medical awards and fifty-four honorary doctorates from universities in the U.S. and abroad. In 1976, she was the first woman to be awarded the Albert Lasker Prize for Basic Medical Research. When Solomon Berson died in 1972, Yalow named her laboratory after him and became its director. She worked as a research professor at Mt. Sinai Hospital School of Medicine from 1968 to 1974.

In 1977 she shared the Nobel Prize in Physiology or Medicine for work involving RIA, thus becoming the first American-born and -educated woman to win this award.

From 1979 to 1985, Yalow was a professor-at-large at the Albert Einstein College of Medicine in New York, and from 1980 to 1985 she was chairperson of the department of clinical science at the Montefiore Hospital and Medical Center in the Bronx. She was awarded the National Medal of Science, the nation's highest award in science, in 1988.

Since retiring from the VA Hospital in 1991, Yalow has been devoting her time to promoting science education and better child care. She has particularly emphasized the need for more scientific training for women. According to Yalow, "The world cannot afford the loss of the talents of half its people if we are to solve the many problems which beset us."

Rosalyn Yalow went against the odds and, through sheer will and dedication, proved that women have a place among the best scientists in the world.

Judith Resnick, the first Jewish astronaut, perished when NASA's space shuttle *Challenger* exploded on January 29, 1986.

The New York Times

VOL. CXXXV... No. 46,669 ... NEW YORK, WEDNESDAY, JANUARY 29, 1986 ... 30 CENTS

THE SHUTTLE EXPLODES

6 IN CREW AND HIGH-SCHOOL TEACHER ARE KILLED 74 SECONDS AFTER LIFTOFF

Thousands Watch A Rain of Debris

From the Beginning to the End

How Could It Happen? Fuel Tank Leak Feared

After the Shock, a Need to Share Grief and Loss

Reagan Lauds 'Heroes'

Francis R. Scobee
Commander

Michael J. Smith
Pilot

Judith A. Resnik
Electrical Engineer

Ellison S. Onizuka

Ronald E. McNair

Gregory B. Jarvis

Christa McAuliffe

92

Chapter Eleven

Women in Literature

More women today distinguish themselves as writers than at any other time in history. Around the world, women—many of them Jewish—have been producing major literary works. One indicator of this phenomenon is the growing number of women writers who have won the Nobel Prize for Literature during the past forty years. Among them are two Jewish women, Nelly Sachs and Nadine Gordimer.

Jewish women have played a prominent role in American literature throughout the twentieth century. One early example is Gertrude Stein, remembered not so much for her own writing as for her profound influence on major American literary figures such as F. Scott Fitzgerald and Ernest Hemingway. Edna Ferber was one of the most popular American novelists of the century, with novels such as *Show Boat* and *Giant*. The first was made into an immensely successful Broadway musical, and the second into a major movie. Lillian Hellman was a leading American playwright known for such plays as *The Children's Hour* and *The Little Foxes*. Among short story

writers, Cynthia Ozick stands out with collections such as *The Pagan Rabbi*. Among historians, Barbara Tuchman is celebrated for books like *The Guns of August*. More recently, Jewish feminist writers like Betty Friedan, author of *The Feminine Mystique*, and Letty Cottin Pogrebin, author of *Deborah, Golda, and Me: Being Female and Jewish in America,* have had a defining influence on the feminist movement and on Jewish feminism, respectively.

In Israel, much of the best prose and poetry has been written by women. Earlier we saw how the poet Ra'hel helped shape the new Hebrew literary idiom, while another woman poet, Dahlia Ravikovitch, recently won the Israel Prize for literature. Other important Israeli poets include Leah Goldberg and Yocheved Bat-Miriam. Shulamit Har-Even and Yehudit Handel are important Israeli novelists. Some of Israel's most beloved folk songs were written by Naomi Shemer, best known for her song "Jerusalem of Gold," which almost became Israel's new national anthem.

The first Jewish woman to win the Nobel Prize for Literature was Nelly Sachs, who in 1966 shared the prize with the Israeli writer Samuel Joseph Agnon. The world knew little about Sachs before the Nobel announcement. Only a privileged few had access to her poetry. But once she became famous, her poems appeared in many languages around the world. Still today, only those truly dedicated to poetry take the time to sift through her imagery and metaphors, which do not easily yield their hidden meaning.

> *O the chimneys*
> *On the cleverly devised dwellings of death*
> *When Israel's body sailed like smoke*
> *Through the air—*
> *Was welcomed by a star, a chimney sweep,*
> *A star turned black*
> *Or was it a sunbeam?*

There are good reasons why Sachs' poetry is not easy to decipher. One must first look at her background, and then at her subject matter. Leonie Nelly Sachs was born in Berlin in 1891 to wealthy German Jewish parents. She was educated by private tutors, and studied music and dance. At a young age she showed a passion for literature, and in her teens she came under the influence of Christian German mysticism and wrote poems and stories influenced by the German mystic and romantic tradition. Some of her work was published.

When Hitler came to power in Germany in 1933, Sachs became deeply aware of her Jewish background and began to

Nelly Sachs

94

study Jewish mysticism. During the 1930s, she lost her entire family to concentration camps, except for her mother. The lives of Sachs and her mother were saved thanks to a friendship Sachs had developed through letters exchanged with the Swedish writer Selma Lagerlöf, one of the greatest writers of the early twentieth century. The aging Lagerlöf was able to secure a Swedish visa for the two women, and in 1940 they arrived in Stockholm as refugees.

For the next quarter century, Sachs dedicated herself to writing about the Holocaust. In 1947 she published her first volume of poetry, *In den Wohnungen des Todes (In the Habitations of Death)*. Her poems, like carefully crafted building blocks, form an edifice of words dedicated to the suffering of the human race, especially that of the Jews. Her German style, modern and abstract, is rich in biblical images, particularly the language of the great prophets of Israel.

Many believe it is impossible to give poetic or artistic expression to the enormity of the Holocaust, the indescribable suffering of millions of human beings, men, women, and children. Has Sachs been able to encompass the Holocaust in her work? Her poem "O the Chimneys" may hold part of the answer. In this poem she informs us that the Holocaust was a tragedy not of individual human beings, but rather of an entire people, or "Israel's body." Echoing the words of the Passover Haggadah, she seems to be saying, "A Jew must look upon him or herself as if he or she were personally freed from Egypt." In other words, the Holocaust happened to all of us. And it was not caused by the Germans alone, but by the world as a whole, who tolerated the existence of the "dwellings of death," namely, the gas chambers and the crematoria with their chimneys turning the sky black with smoke of human ashes.

The judges who awarded Nelly Sachs the Nobel Prize gave the following reason:

> With moving intensity of feeling she has given voice to the worldwide tragedy of the Jewish people, which she has expressed in lyrical laments of painful beauty and in dramatic legends. Her symbolic language body combines an inspired modern idiom with echoes of ancient biblical poetry. Identifying herself totally with the faith and ritual mysticism of her people, Miss Sachs has created a world of imagery, which does not shun the terrible truths of the extermination camps and corpse factories, but which at the same time rises above all hatred of the persecutors, merely revealing a genuine sorrow at man's debasement.

*But who emptied your shoes of sand
When you had to get up, to die?
The sand which Israel gathered,
Its nomad sand?
Burning Sinai sand,
Mingled with throats of nightingales,
Mingled with wings of butterflies.*
—Nelly Sachs

Nadine Gordimer

In the decades since World War II, thousands of Jewish women who survived the Holocaust have written their memoirs of that darkest of nights. Many have also tried to express themselves in story, art, and poetry. But the work of Nelly Sachs continues to tower as a monument of poetic depth and dignity to the memory of those to whom she dedicated her first volume of poems with the words, "To my dead brothers and sisters."

❧ ❧ ❧

Nadine Gordimer is recognized as one of the most important writers in the world at the close of the twentieth century. She was born in 1923 in a small mining town near Johannesburg, South Africa. Her father was an Orthodox Jew from Lithuania, and her mother, descended from generations of English Jews, was completely non-observant. As a result, Nadine grew up in a conflicted home which gave her no reason to embrace her Jewish heritage. Years later, when it was suggested to her that her zeal for social justice came from her Jewish background, she rejected the notion. Her cultural orientation certainly was not Jewish.

Unlike Nelly Sachs, whose life was completely reshaped by the Holocaust, Gordimer's life was shaped by one of the most tragically racist regimes of modern times, the Apartheid regime of South Africa, in which nonwhite South Africans had few or no rights. She started writing at age nine, and her first story was published in a South African magazine when she was fifteen. Her first collection of short stories, *Face to Face*, was published ten years later in 1949. Her first novel, *The Lying Days*, was issued in 1953.

In later books Gordimer sought to show how Apartheid was destroying the moral fiber of South African society. Three of her novels, starting with *A World of Strangers*, published in 1958, were subsequently banned in her own country. Gordimer became part of an unofficial, worldwide confederacy of persecuted writers who suffered because of their determination to tell the truth as they saw it. Nevertheless, she did not leave her native South Africa. She did, however, travel extensively and lecture all over the world. She also taught in several U.S. universities during the 1960s and '70s.

In 1991 Gordimer was awarded the Nobel Prize for Literature. In her Nobel Lecture she spoke about the artist's search for truth and the plight of writers shunned or even persecuted in their native land. She said:

I return from the horrific singular threat [on the life of Iranian writer Salman Rushdie by his own government] to those that have been general for writers of this century now in its final, summing-up decade. In repressive regimes anywhere—whether in what was the Soviet bloc, Latin America, Africa, China—most imprisoned writers have been shut away for their activities as citizens striving for liberation against the oppression of the general society to which they belong. Others have been condemned by repressive regimes for serving society by writing as well as they can; for this aesthetic venture of ours becomes subversive when the shameful secrets of our times are explored deeply, with the artist's rebellious integrity to the state of being manifest in life around her or him; then the writer's themes and characters inevitably are formed by the pressures and distortions of that society as the life of the fisherman is determined by the power of the sea.

She concluded her speech by saying:

The writer is of service to humankind only insofar as the writer uses the word even against his or her own loyalties, trusts the state of being, as it is revealed, to hold somewhere in its complexity filaments of the cord of truth, able to be bound together, here and there, in art: trusts the state of being to yield somewhere fragmentary phrases of truth, which is the final word of words, never changed by our stumbling efforts to spell it out and write it down, never changed by lies, by semantic sophistry, by the dirtying of the word for the purpose of racism, sexism, prejudice, domination, the glorification of destruction, the curses and the praise-songs.

First page of the Book of Ruth

Chapter Twelve

Women on Stage and Screen

Historically, Jews did not cultivate drama and other forms of audiovisual entertainment to the same extent as Greek and Roman cultures did. Nevertheless, there is great drama in the Bible and in Jewish culture in general, and the emotional aspect of Judaism is well developed. Beginning in the nineteenth century, Jews began to take an active part in the theater. Jewish actors like Rachel Felix and Sarah Bernhardt dominated the French stage during that period. At the turn of the century, the Yiddish theater, which started in Europe, came to the United States (mainly New York) with the large waves of Jewish immigrants. It produced outstanding actors, some of whom made the transition into English-speaking American stage and motion pictures. A few examples are Sophie Tucker, Fanny Brice, and Molly Picon.

Throughout the twentieth century, Jews made a vast contribution to the American entertainment industry in such areas as vaudeville, comedy, music, drama, radio, motion pictures, and television. Some of the best known Jewish performers are Beverly Sills, Roberta Peters, Shelly Winters, Claire Bloom, Esther Williams, Dinah Shore, Ida Kaminska, Lilli Palmer, Luise Rainer, Jill St. John, Joan Rivers, Lauren Bacall, Judy Holliday, Bette Midler, Barbra Streisand, Elaine May, Goldie Hawn, and Debra Winger; other well known performers, including Norma Shearer, Marilyn Monroe, and Elizabeth Taylor, converted to Judaism. In this chapter we will take a look at three Jewish performers whose combined careers cover almost a full century of American entertainment.

Molly Picon did it all. Her career, spanning almost the entire twentieth century, reads like the history of the Yiddish stage in America, as well as the early history of vaudeville, radio,

Yiddish was our center, our link. I never felt like a complete stranger in Europe because I was always in the midst of a familiar language and heritage—the Yiddish world.
—Molly Picon

motion pictures, and more. She performed for nearly eighty years, from the first years of the twentieth century to 1992. Hers is undoubtedly one of the most remarkable stories of both Jewish and American culture in the twentieth century.

Because Molly Picon was considered the first lady of the Yiddish theater, many people thought she had been born in Europe and spoke Yiddish. This was not so. She was born in New York in 1898 and spoke English as a child. Her mother worked as a seamstress for a Yiddish theater company, and at age five Molly started performing dance and song numbers in Yiddish. She was a tiny and vivacious child with wide eyes and a small round face, and she would retain her childish charm well into her older years.

Molly Picon, the "Queen of the Yiddish Stage," began performing as a young girl.

The first four decades of the twentieth century were the golden years of the Yiddish stage in America. American show business and the Yiddish theater are closely intertwined. Jews played a very prominent role in developing the American movie industry, the Broadway stage, American comedy, radio entertainment, and later television. Many Jewish performers had their start on the Yiddish stage, and some, like Molly Picon, made the transition to the English-speaking stage and screen.

In those years, most Jews in America were immigrants whose native language was Yiddish. Their ancestors in Europe had spoken Yiddish, a mixture of old German and Hebrew, for nearly five hundred years. While not a fully developed language with fixed grammatical rules, Yiddish is a very expressive and dramatic tongue, rich in words expressing feelings and humor, and able to convey perhaps better than any other language great joy as well as deep sorrow and pain. American English has borrowed many Yiddish expressions from that period, including *chutzpah*, *klutz*, and *shtick*.

During World War II, most of Europe's Yiddish-speaking Jews perished in the Holocaust. In America, first- and second-generation, native-born American Jews were no longer taught Yiddish, so few could speak it. After the war, audiences at Yiddish theaters in New York and elsewhere began to dwindle, and nearly all of those theaters have since disappeared. Nevertheless, Yiddish had a significant impact on American popular culture.

In 1919, when Picon married a Yiddish theater manager named Jacob Kalich, her stage career was launched. Applying her singing, dancing, acting, and comic talents to the Yiddish musical stage, she became one of its leading stars. In 1921 Kalich took Picon to Europe to expand her career in the great Yiddish theaters of the "Old Country." She performed throughout Europe, from Paris to Kishinev and from London to Bucharest, and enchanted audiences everywhere. So began her lifelong reputation throughout the Yiddish-speaking world as the greatest Yiddish performer.

During the 1920s and '30s, Picon performed all over the world—in America, Europe, South America, and South Africa. One of the major themes of her plays and films was the growing gap between American and European Jews. While American Jewry was coming into its own, European Jewry was declining. In 1937 Picon went to Poland to film a Yiddish comedy called *Yidel mitn Fidl (Yiddle with the Fiddle)*, the story of a young girl who dresses up as a boy so she and her father can earn a living as *klezmers*, or roving musicians. For a wedding scene in the movie, the studio hired a group of Orthodox Jews from the local Polish town. Picon writes in her memoir:

Molly Picon appears on the stage in Paris, 1920.

> The wedding scene . . . took over thirty consecutive hours to film. The food had to be truly kosher, because we hired Orthodox Jewish men, women, and children of Kazimierez to be guests. As we filmed, they ate, and for the successive shots of the table, the food had to be replenished, over and over again . . . Our poverty stricken guests couldn't figure out what was happening. They thought they had been invited to a real wedding . . .

Yiddle with the Fiddle became a classic and can still be seen on video. The next year Kalich and Picon returned to Poland to film *Mamale (Mommy)*, a musical comedy which was the last Jewish film made in Poland before the Nazi onslaught. At forty, Picon played a girl of twelve whose mother died and left her to take care of her large and unappreciative family. The film took on special poignancy as she and Kalich struggled to capture the endangered shtetl culture on the eve of World War II.

Picon with Barbra Streisand in *For Pete's Sake*, 1971

During the war, Picon performed at many U.S. military bases all over the United States and Canada. When the war ended, Picon traveled to Europe to perform for Jewish survivors. It was to her the most important thing she ever did. She

101

Posters in English and Yiddish
announcing a performance by
Picon and Kalich, 1949

was able to make people who had not laughed in seven years laugh again for the first time. During the postwar years, she devoted much of her time to work on Jewish causes, helping settle war refugees, revive interest in Yiddish culture, and raise money for the new Jewish state. In 1954 Picon was honored by the United Jewish Appeal for her fundraising activities. She made her first trip to Israel that year and gave benefit performances for the Jewish National Fund and the Red Magen David, and was even invited to sing for the Israeli Knesset.

In the 1960s Picon, now in her sixties, started a Hollywood career in major American films. She was Frank Sinatra's Italian mother in the movie *Come Blow Your Horn,* for which she received an Oscar nomination. She also starred on Broadway in the musical *Milk and Honey*, in which she played a widow looking for a husband in Israel.

In 1979, at age eighty-one, Picon created her one-woman show, *Hello Molly,* and took it on the road. The show traced her long and loving relationship with the Yiddish theater and gave her an opportunity to remain connected to her beloved audiences.

When Picon died in 1992 at age ninety-four, it seemed that her legacy as one of the greatest Yiddish performers of all time had receded into the past and might be forgotten. This, however, has not been the case. There is renewed interest in Yiddish culture and language, and Picon's contributions, preserved in print and on film, will continue to enrich the lives of future generations.

❦   ❦   ❦

If Molly Picon represents the immigrant generation of Jewish entertainers in America, Lauren Bacall is prototypical of the American-born generation. This was a generation that had cut most of its ties to Judaism. Most no longer spoke Yiddish, did not attend synagogue, and blended into the American mainstream. In fact, most people, including Jews, are surprised to discover that movie stars like Tony Curtis, Kirk Douglas, Jill St. John, and Lauren Bacall are Jews who originally had Jewish names. While many members of this generation had little or nothing to do with Jewish life, after the Holocaust and the birth of the State of Israel nearly all of them had a change of heart about their Judaism. They became more open about their Jewish roots, began to support Jewish causes, and in some instances took leadership positions in the Jewish community.

Lauren Bacall

What many of them had in common were their humble origins. Most came from working class immigrant families. They grew up either on the Lower East Side of New York or in Brooklyn or in other poor neighborhoods of American cities. Since most of them could not afford higher education, they relied on their good looks and artistic skills to become entertainers, and some of them even achieved stardom in Hollywood.

One of those actors was Lauren Bacall, whose looks and acting style made her one of Hollywood's best known and most glamorous stars.

Bacall's name was Betty Perske when she was born in New York City in 1924. When she was three, her mother sent her to dance school, hoping her daughter would find fame and fortune as a performer. At age ten, Bacall's parents were divorced, her father disappeared from her life, and her mother had to take a secretarial job to support the two of them. That was when Bacall realized she would have to make her own way in the world, and she did.

As a teenager, Bacall dreamed of a movie career. One of the great screen idols in those days was Humphrey Bogart. Bacall's special dream was to act in one of Bogart's movies. While many teenagers had such dreams, Bacall made it a reality, perhaps beyond her wildest dreams.

At nineteen, while playing a small part on Broadway, Bacall

was discovered by a fashion magazine editor. Later that year (1943) her face appeared on the cover of *Harper's Bazaar*. Her poise and her bewitching look opened the door to Hollywood. A year later, when she was barely twenty and had little acting experience, she was given a part opposite Humphrey Bogart in the movie *To Have and Have Not*.

In true Hollywood fashion, Bacall fell in love, and although Bogart was more than twice her age, they got married. For twelve years, until Bogart's death in 1957, Bogart and Bacall were one of Hollywood's most celebrated couples. During that time Bacall made several movies with her husband, the best known of which are *The Big Sleep* (1946) and *Key Largo* (1948). Still in her early twenties, she had become one of Hollywood's big stars.

Bacall continued acting well into her seventies but never reached the level of her early successes with Bogart. After Bogart died, she had a brief romance with Frank Sinatra, and from 1961 to 1967 she was married to Jason Robards. But it appears that Bogart always remained the love of her life.

In 1959 she returned to Broadway, and for the next twenty-two years acted successfully in plays such as *Cactus Flower*, *Applause*, and *Woman of the Year*, winning Tony awards for the last two. In her memoirs, written in 1979, Bacall speaks about her Jewish origins. She describes the strength and warmth she found in Jewish family life despite her parents' early divorce and her father's leaving the family when she was little.

In 1996 Bacall's movie career was revived when she played Barbra Streisand's mother in the film *The Mirror Has Two Faces*. There is something symbolic about this movie: In many ways, Bacall represents the second generation of Hollywood movie stars of Jewish origin, while Streisand represents the third. Appearing together in this movie, they bring the story of Jewish women in Hollywood full circle.

❧   ❧   ❧

Many consider Barbra Streisand the greatest entertainer of our time. It seems appropriate that the story of Jewish women on stage and screen in the twentieth century, which starts with Molly Picon, culminates with Barbra Streisand. For Streisand is living proof that one can be an accomplished and universally popular performer and at the same time be a positive and proud Jew, without making any apologies for one's eth-

Going back through my life now, the Jewish family feeling stands proud and strong, and at least I can say I am glad I sprang from that.
—Lauren Bacall

nic or religious background.

Like Molly Picon and Lauren Bacall, Barbra Streisand experienced a difficult childhood. In Barbra's case, her father died when she was fifteen, and her mother had to work to support her family. As a teenager, Barbra was comfortable with both her Judaism and her performing skills. She belonged to the Jewish youth organization B'nai B'rith Girls (BBG), and she knew she was going to be either a singer or an actor. Her mother wasn't so sure, since Barbra did not quite fit the American stereotype of beauty of that time. But upon graduation with honors from high school, Barbra moved to Manhattan and started her relentless pursuit of a career in show business.

She had much to show for herself. She could sing, she could act, and she was very funny. Those attributes got her a role in the Broadway musical *I Can Get It for You Wholesale* before she was even twenty. Her part in the show won her the New York Drama Critics Award for 1962. She was now on her way to stardom.

In 1964 she won great fame in one of Broadway's all-time hits, *Funny Girl*. She played the lead role, portraying Fanny Brice, another versatile Jewish woman entertainer whom she greatly admired. Two songs from this show—"People" and "Don't Rain on My Parade"—were enormous hits and established Streisand as one of the most popular singers of her time. The movie version of *Funny*

Courtesy of *The Washington Jewish Week*

Barbra Streisand

Courtesy of *The Washington Jewish Week*

Barbra Streisand with the late Prime Minister of Israel, Yitzhak Rabin, and his wife, Leah

Girl won her an Oscar as best actress.

Streisand went on to become one of Hollywood's greatest stars. Her early movies include *Hello Dolly* (1969), *The Owl and the Pussycat* (1970), and *The Way We Were* (1973).

Searching for her Jewish roots, Streisand decided in 1983 to produce a movie in the tradition of the old Yiddish films. She selected *Yentl,* a story by the Yiddish writer Isaac Bashevis Singer about a young woman in Eastern Europe who wants to study in a rabbinical academy and must disguise herself as a boy to be accepted. Bringing this kind of theme before a movie-going public with little interest in the subject matter was no easy task. Streisand decided to take full responsibility for the film and became the first woman ever to produce, direct, write, and star in a major motion picture. It turned out to be an important cultural event and a successful film.

Despite her great success, Barbra had her share of personal challenges. Her first marriage, to actor Elliott Gould, ended in divorce after six years. In mid-life she developed a fear of performing before large audiences, and it took her nearly thirty years to return to the concert stage. When she finally did in 1994, thousands of delighted fans attended her concerts.

While becoming the biggest-selling female recording artist ever, Streisand continued to make movies. In 1996 she released the movie *The Mirror Has Two Faces*, in which Lauren Bacall plays her mother.

While leading a busier life than most people in or out of movies, Streisand has always found time for liberal, humanitarian, and Jewish causes. A lifelong liberal Democrat, she has campaigned for U.S. Presidents from Lyndon Johnson to Bill Clinton. She has fought for gay rights and has always been vocal on issues concerning women's rights. For years, she has been a staunch supporter of the State of Israel, and when Israel signed a peace treaty with Jordan, Prime Minister Yitzhak Rabin invited Ms. Streisand to the signing ceremony. In 1997 she agreed to serve as honorary chair of the Brandeis University center for the study of Jewish women.

Molly Picon, Lauren Bacall, and Barbra Streisand—in many ways so different from one another, and yet so similar—brought joy and inspiration to millions. Through their artistic achievements they will continue to enrich people's lives for a long time to come.

Chapter Thirteen

Women in Art

The story of Jewish women in art history is similar to that of all women in this field: They have been noticeably absent. For many years, historians believed that women were not among the most famous artists because women did not have the required talent. This idea has been challenged and dismantled in contemporary thinking about art. In the last thirty years, a branch of art criticism specifically devoted to feminist concerns has investigated these issues.

In 1971, an art historian named Linda Nochlin, herself Jewish, wrote a famous essay entitled "Why Have There Been No Great Women Artists?" In this essay, Nochlin points out a variety of reasons why women have not been among the so-called great artists. She shows how historically, women did not have access to the means to become professional artists. Women did not have time free from their domestic responsibilities to be artists, women were not admitted into art classes because it was considered improper for a woman to draw from a nude model, and it was simply unacceptable to exhibit a painting with a woman's signature. In fact, some of art history's most famous paintings were painted by women who actually signed their father's or husband's name to the works.

Sculpture by Chana Orloff, an early Israeli artist

The task of uncovering and seeking such work by women is referred to as "revisionist history." Such histories have examined domestic articles such as quilts and needlepoint samplers as examples of art work by women. An example of revisionist history can be seen in the next chapter, which shows how the production of ritual objects provided a means for Jewish women to be involved in visually creative pursuits.

Since the advent of modern art, women have played an increasingly important role in the field of visual arts, and Jewish women have been among the most important of these artists. Prior to the feminist movement of the late 1960s, many of these women's accomplishments were overshadowed by those of their husbands. Lee Krasner was a Jewish artist married to Jackson Pollack, a founder of the Abstract Expressionist art movement. Louise Bourgeois, Susan Rothenberg, and Helen Frankenthaler also worked during this period. Additionally, art produced outside of Europe or the United States often does not receive as much attention as that produced within these areas. Chana Orloff, an Israeli woman whose sculptures fit within a style most often exemplified by the work of the English sculptor Henry Moore, has gotten little attention outside of Israel.

Since the early 1970s, when the feminist movement sought to create a more inclusive version of art, women have become more visible in art than ever before. Many of the most influential women artists of this era were Jewish, including Judy Chicago, Eva Hesse, Carolee Schneeman, Rachel Rosenthal, Mierle Ukeles, and Hannah Wilke. Hannah Wilke was an artist who worked mainly in the late 1960s and early 1970s. Through her work, she sought to create a specifically feminine form of imagery. She accomplished this by turning everyday objects and materials, such as lint and chewing gum, into small abstract sculptures representing women's bodies and sexualities. Wilke also produced several bodies of work on specifically Jewish themes, such as *Venus Pareve* (1982-84), in which the artist examines her own Jewish body in relation to that of the cultural ideal of Venus.

I Shop Therefore I Am, by Barbara Kruger.

During the 1980s, a new art movement called post-modernism began. A Jewish woman named Barbara Kruger is among the most important post-modern artists, male or female. Kruger began her career as a graphic designer and subsequently applied this style to her fine art works, which have taken the form of photographs, installations (a kind of art work that occupies a whole room), and billboards. She combines images taken directly from advertising with text to comment on the major role of mass media (such as television and magazines) in contemporary life. The image illustrated here, *I Shop Therefore I Am*, also employs humor to criticize how much of our identity is based on the material goods that we own. This piece was printed on t-shirts and shopping bags for the Museum of Modern Art in New York City, furthering the association of art with advertising and breaking down assumptions of the place of art in culture.

108

Jewish women have also been involved in experimental art media such as video and film. Lynn Hershman and Martha Rosler were among the first women to use video as an art medium in the 1970s. Other experimental film makers, such as Beth B and Lisa Lewenz, have used film and video as a medium to examine issues surrounding the history of the Holocaust.

The discussion of Jewish women in art is limited mainly to the contemporary period, a fact which is true generally for women in art history. As Linda Nochlin stated in 1971, in the past "it was indeed institutionally *impossible* for women to achieve excellence or success on the same footing as men, no matter what their talent, or genius." This position has been doubly difficult for Jewish women, who were limited in their career options not only as a result of their gender but also as a result of their religion and culture. Historically, Jewish religion and culture considered art a frivolous pursuit for men (only a few Jewish men were recognized as artists) and inappropriate for women.

Increasingly, both Jewish artists and work on Jewish themes have become acceptable in the art world. In 1996, The Jewish Museum in New York City mounted perhaps the largest ever contemporary exhibition on Jewish themes. For the exhibition, titled "Too Jewish? Challenging Traditional Identities," curator Norman Kleeblatt included many Jewish women artists, among them Deborah Kass, Cary Leibowitz, Rhonda Lieberman, Beverly Naidus, Rona Pondick, Ilene Segalove, and Hannah Wilke. Linda Nochlin wrote a foreword for the exhibition catalogue. The major role of these women in this exhibition shows that, just as Jews have found their way into all aspects of contemporary life, and just as women have begun to find their way into contemporary art, so too have Jewish women started to claim their place and make their voices heard as artists.

❧ ❧ ❧

Judy Chicago is one of the most important figures in the history of feminist art. She began working in the early 1970s, fueled by her desire to eradicate sexism in the arts. She and a group of other feminist artists, including Miriam Schapiro, began using imagery which they felt to be specifically feminine, and incorporating materials which had historically been considered "female," such as needlework and quilting. These women helped found an art school for feminist studies at the

[In the past] it was indeed institutionally impossible *for women to achieve excellence or success on the same footing as men, no matter what their talent, or genius.*
—Linda Nochlin

California Institute of the Arts. Their work has led to greater inclusion and acceptance of feminist art in the art world.

In the late 1970s, Ms. Chicago produced *The Dinner Party.* This multimedia art work includes place settings for thirty-nine women who were major figures in the history of Western civilization but had previously been left out of history texts. The piece represents a major effort of revisionist history to relocate these women and make their accomplishments known. *The Birth Project,* Chicago's next major work, includes over eighty pieces, all executed under the supervision of skilled needleworkers. The project focuses on the birth process.

For *The Holocaust Project,* Judy Chicago treats a Jewish theme. Chicago grew up as an assimilated Jew and as a young girl did not learn much about Jewish history. As an adult she was drawn into investigating feminism and the history of women. Eventually, her desire to learn about the oppression of women led to her desire to learn more about the historical oppression of Jews. *The Holocaust Project* is a major series of art pieces—tapestries, stained glass, and paintings—which chronicles Ms. Chicago's experiences as she learns about the Holocaust. Produced in collaboration with her husband, Donald Woodman, this project was exhibited in 1993 at the Spertus Museum of Judaica in Chicago, Illinois. *The Holocaust Project* encompasses a major and vast topic in Jewish history from a specifically feminist point of view. In Chicago's own words, "The goal of *The Holocaust Project* is to reach a wide and diverse audience, to stimulate dialogue and heighten awareness about the world in which we live, and to offer hope that we can create a more peaceful world."

❧   ❧   ❧

Deborah Kass is a young contemporary Jewish artist. She grew up in the suburbs of New York and currently lives in New York City. Her work has been exhibited widely in galleries and museums, most notably in the exhibition "Too Jewish? Challenging Traditional Identities" at The Jewish Museum in New York City.

Many of Deborah Kass's paintings make reference to the work of Andy Warhol, an important American artist. Warhol is known for his paintings of American pop culture icons, or celebrities—like Marilyn Monroe and Jackie Kennedy Onassis—who have come to stand for American values. Warhol's work was part of a movement called Pop Art, which sought to elevate facets of everyday life to worthwhile topics for artists. He often worked with repeated images taken directly from magazines, newspapers, and other widely available sources.

In her paintings of *The Jewish Jackie* series, Deborah Kass uses Andy Warhol's style but uses Barbra Streisand as her symbol. In so doing, Kass both points out the lack of Jews among American idols and also introduces one onto the list. Since she was a teenager, Kass has been drawn to Barbra Streisand. By using Streisand as a subject in her art, Kass acknowledges Streisand's importance in American culture. Additionally, Barbra Streisand appears in profile in the paintings, emphasizing the physical characteristic that is most particularly Jewish about her: her nose. By making Streisand's nose a prominent feature in her imagery, Ms. Kass encourages us to be proud of our bodies, though they may not fit the ideal of mainstream Gentile culture.

Another of Deborah Kass's paintings features Streisand in her role in the film *Yentl*. In this film set in Eastern Europe before World War II, Streisand plays a young Jewish woman who dresses as a man in order to be able to study the Talmud. Ms. Kass's reference to this particular role acknowledges Streisand's contribution to challenging gender stereotypes and sexism in Jewish history.

Kass's attraction to Streisand stems from her ability to see this Jewish woman as a role model. Streisand is often thought of as a woman with *chutzpah*, a Jewish woman who became successful in Hollywood against the odds of her ethnicity. As Deborah Kass stated in an interview in the *Village Voice:*

> For me, at twelve years old, looking at Barbra, who looked completely different than any other Broadway or Hollywood star, I was very aware of what distinguished her from other "glamorous" women. It was her intelligence, her talent, and her "difference," her ethnicity. She didn't look like Marilyn Monroe, she looked like a Jewish girl from New York. I identified. It was exhilarating for me.

Feminist art criticism has centered around the notion that the images we see in art influence the way we feel not only about others but also about ourselves. When we see an image of Marilyn Monroe, we come to believe that being like Marilyn Monroe is something we should aspire to. By elevating Barbra Streisand to this same level, Deborah Kass encourages Jewish women to be proud of who they are and to see greater opportunity for themselves in contemporary society.

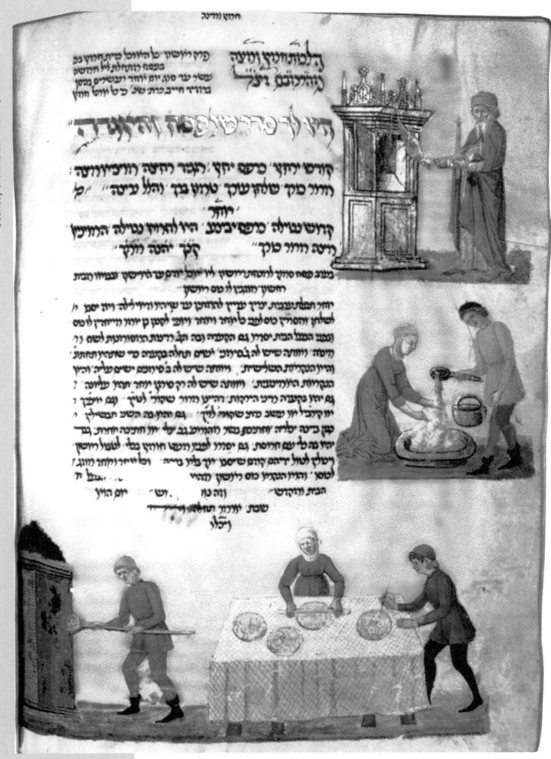

Women preparing for Passover. Detail from
the Rothschild Manuscript, sixteenth century.

"Treblinka/Genocide" (panel)
from the *Holocaust Project* by Judy Chicago

Sabbath Table, by Malcah Zeldis

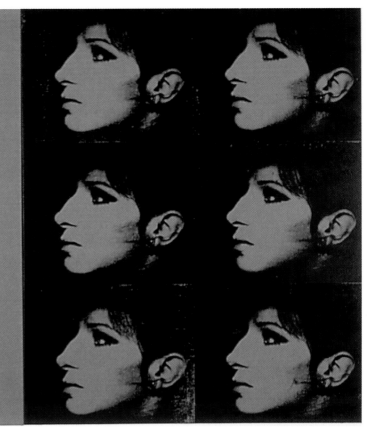

"Double Blue Barbra" from the *Jewish Jackie Series* by Deborah Kass, 1992. Acrylic on canvas

Triple Silver Yentl by Deborah Kass, 1993. Silkscreen ink and acrylic on canvas

Chapter Fourteen

Women in Jewish Ritual Art

The Jewish tradition of making beautiful and functional ritual objects for use in worship began with Bezalel, the son of Uri. The Hebrew Bible tells us that Bezalel was entrusted with the fabrication of the ceremonial instruments and textiles for the Tabernacle of the ancient Temple in Jerusalem. He is described as being "endowed . . . with a divine spirit of skill, ability, and knowledge in every kind of craft" (Exodus 31:3).

The act of enhancing a ritual by making or even commissioning a fine, ceremonial object is called *hiddur mitzvah*, or "glorifying the commandment." This process is understood as a way to glorify God, and it creates a special connection between the maker and the custom or ceremony.

Historically, women have been exempted from regular participation in communal worship, segregated in the sanctuary, and excluded from leadership roles in communal prayer. Yet many women did find a way to participate and to be strongly invested in communal prayers and life cycle events: They used their expertise to make ritual objects for use both in the synagogue and the home.

Although many of their names have been unrecorded or forgotten, women have played an important role in the realm of Jewish ritual art.

Courtesy of Lia Lynn Rosen

New Moon Bowl by Lia Lynn Rosen, Albuquerque, New Mexico (1993). This is a new type of ritual object, created for use by women in new moon ceremonies.

113

They predominantly made textiles, rather than objects in other media, for ritual use. Objects used for customs and ceremonies outside the sanctuary included domestic linens, such as decorative tablecloths embroidered with blessings recited before and after a meal, and bread covers for festival feasts. Other types of objects include *mezuzah* covers and burial shrouds.

While synagogue textiles were not fabricated or donated exclusively by women, we know of many instances where this was the case. Textiles made for the sanctuary include lectern covers, curtains for the Torah Ark, and mantles and binders for covering and securing the Torah scrolls. The custom of women making textile Torah ornaments was so prevalent in Italy that a specific prayer was spoken to acknowledge their contributions. This prayer is still found in the Roman liturgy:

> *May the One who blessed our matriarchs, Sarah, Rebecca, Rachel, and Leah, bless every daughter of Israel who makes a mantle or cover in honor of the Torah . . . May the Holy One reward her and repay her kindness.*

Sometimes, women presented a beautiful textile to the synagogue in honor of an event of personal importance, such as a wedding or death. This gave women a way to make their presence felt in the local Jewish community. Many of the textiles that have survived are boldly emblazoned with the names of the donors, and an item such as a Torah Ark curtain would have been prominently displayed in the sanctuary. These inscriptions tell us whether the female donors were married, unmarried, or widowed. A gift might have given the donor certain privileges, such as a guarantee that *yizkor* memorial prayers would be said after her death, in order that her name be remembered.

The style of a ritual textile would vary greatly according to the community or region of origin. Usually, however, the finest fabrics available were utilized, ranging from a sumptuous silk in a wealthy, urban Italian community to a simple, printed cotton in a small German village. The fabrication of the piece was a source of creative enrichment for the maker. Sometimes, a group of women would work together on an elaborate Torah Ark curtain *(parokhet)*, or a new mother would make a Torah binder *(wimpel)* from the cloth on which her son was circumcised. Embroidery techniques were handed down through generations of women and were part of a young girl's education. A few eighteenth- and nineteenth-century samplers have survived, embroidered with alphabets in both English and Hebrew scripts. These show that while young Jewish women learned the art of needlework, they also learned to read in both languages.

※   ※   ※

Beginning in the twentieth century, there has been a reevaluation of the role of women in Jewish ritual life. Women are now recognized as rabbis and equal participants in communal worship in the American Conservative and Reform movements. Women have been instrumental in creating new liturgy, rituals, and even ritual objects in areas where a lack has been felt.

As women have taken on different roles in the community, their involvement in fabricating objects for ceremonial use has all but disappeared. Yet women are becoming more aware of their unique historical connection to worship. Community projects are being established, individuals are making their own ritual objects for personal use, and highly accomplished, professional women Judaica artists are emerging in all media.

Flower-shaped spice box (silver) for Havdalah
ceremonies, by Paula Newman (1997)

Torah ark curtain by Leah, wife of Hananiah Oto. Italy, 1698-99. Silk embroidery on linen. 184 x 125.5 cm.
The Jewish Museum, New York

Torah binder by Honorata, wife of Samuel Foa. Italy, 1582-83. Linen embroidered with silk threads. 19 x 285 cm. Gift of Dr. Harry G. Friedman. The Jewish Museum, New York. This is one of the earliest surviving Italian Torah binders extant.

Hebrew month Torah binders, by Leslie Colomb Hartman, Pittsburgh, 1993. Created to honor religious school Hebrew holidays. Congregation Beth Shalom, Pittsburgh. Through the Temple Sisterhood, twenty Torah binders have been created.

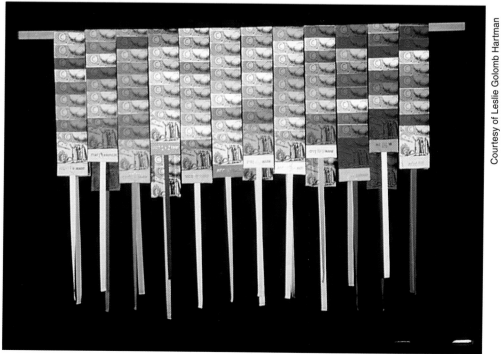

Chapter Fifteen

Women in Business

Over the centuries, Jews were barred from many professions and from owning land, and were forced to engage in a variety of business activities, mostly on a small scale. Many were shopkeepers, others were tailors or shoemakers, and still others became traders or merchants. In many of those activities there was a need for help, and women often provided it. Earlier we saw how certain women, like Doña Gracia Nasi in the sixteenth century and Glueckel of Hameln in the seventeenth, were highly successful businesswomen. Usually, however, women had to stay in the background while men headed the business.

Women have come a long way since this time. In the twentieth century, certain Jewish women, particularly in the Western world, developed highly successful businesses and business careers. Full equality for women in the business world had not yet been achieved even at the end of this century. But great progress was made, and today many women head major corporations and compete successfully in the marketplace. Here we will take a look at two highly successful Jewish businesswomen who have revolutionized the world's cosmetics industry—Helena Rubinstein and Estée Lauder.

For many years, the name "Helena Rubinstein" has been synonymous with cosmetics worldwide. From Tokyo to Buenos Aires, from New York to Paris, this name is associated with beauty and elegance. Behind the name is a small, sturdy Jewish woman from Poland with a Greek profile, an iron will, and a genius for marketing. In her field, she exemplified the pioneering spirit, doing things that had never been done before. Her life reads like a textbook description of the perfect business person. She was the best in her field.

Helena Rubinstein

Born to a poor family in Cracow, Poland in 1872, Helena was the oldest of eight daughters. A restless spirit, she left Poland in 1902 and went to live with her uncle in Australia. There she became aware of the poor condition of women's skin due to the harsh, dry climate. Helena's mother had a formula for cold cream which Helena herself used in Australia, and soon she began to share it with local women. Realizing its commercial potential, she began to market it. It was an instant success.

She opened a beauty salon in Melbourne, and in three years her hard work paid off. What made Rubinstein so successful was her personal attention to her clients and her realization that different women needed different creams, depending on their skin type. She began to develop different kinds of creams and kept her various formulas a secret.

Rubinstein soon realized she had the potential to change the way women everywhere took care of their skin. When the Australian market became too small for her, she decided to move to London, where she would be at the center of world business. She was advised against it, since British women at that time tended to be conservative and resist change. But she was confident she could change their habits.

And change them she did. In 1908 London saw the opening of Europe's first twentieth-century beauty salon, named "Helena Rubinstein." Two of Rubinstein's sisters were employed in the business, which had now become a family affair. Helena was the undisputed brain, and soon she began to open branches in other parts of the city.

In 1912 she entered the high fashion and cultural capital of the world when she opened a shop in Paris. Soon she became known throughout Europe. Among her Parisian clients were the most fashionable French women of the day, including stage legend Sarah Bernhardt. It was in Paris that Rubinstein acquired her lifelong passion for art, becoming a world-class collector of fine art pieces.

When World War I broke out in 1914, Helena Rubinstein moved her operation to New York, where she found fertile ground for her work. Since American women knew little about skin care and cosmetics at that time, she had her work cut out for her. She proceeded to develop a host of new products, including waterproof mascara and medicated facial creams. Among her marketing innovations was sending saleswomen on the road with her products, thus creating a model for the entire American cosmetics industry. Rubinstein was well on her way to becoming the most successful Jewish business-woman in America.

During the Great Depression of 1929, when many American businesses collapsed, Rubinstein bought back at a low price a large share of her business which she had sold to Lehman Brothers. This enabled her to survive the Depression. Over and over, she showed how the secret of success in business is turning adversity into gain.

After World War II, Helena Rubinstein expanded, opening branches as well as manufacturing facilities worldwide. Thanks to her success, for the first time cosmetics became available to vast numbers of less affluent women.

Now heading a vast cosmetics empire, Rubinstein became a patron of the arts, supporting museums and artists. Today her foundation focuses on supporting women in science. In 1958 she went to Israel to start a cosmetics industry. While there, she became a patron of the Tel Aviv Museum, which established the Helena Rubinstein Pavilion. By the time she died at age ninety-two, Rubinstein was a legend. When asked once how she had attained such success, her answer was, "chutzpah." She had that, and a great deal more.

❦   ❦   ❦

Estée Lauder

The name Estée Lauder is known to any person who has ever walked into a shopping mall. It stands for one of the finest lines of women's cosmetics. Behind the name is a woman who was born in the beginning of the twentieth century. Contrary to popular belief, Estée Lauder was not a countess or the daughter of millionaires. Instead, she was Josephine Esther Mentzer, born in Queens to a Jewish immigrant family. Just like other women who were not afraid to reach out and take risks, she achieved great success in the business world, starting from the bottom and creating one of the most successful companies in her field.

Like Helena Rubinstein before her, Lauder discovered skin-care products at an early age, when the industry was still young. Thanks to a chemist uncle involved in developing such products, as a child Lauder took great interest in improving their quality.

In her twenties Lauder began to work in a beauty salon in uptown Manhattan. Meanwhile, she kept improving her own products, and soon she expanded her activities to homes and hotels, where she provided personal skin care. As she made a name for herself as an expert in her field, she began to develop her own business.

Lauder turned out to be a marketing genius. One of her business innovations was distributing free samples of her products at large gathering, such as charity events. Her products quickly became known to large numbers of people, and demand for her cosmetics began to grow. Estée and her husband, Joseph Lauder, worked out of a small shop in New York, doing everything from making the cream to packaging and delivering it themselves. Soon the most fashionable stores in New York, including Saks Fifth Avenue, began to order their products. The Lauders were now on their way to becoming a household name in cosmetics.

By 1950, Estée Lauder products had become a familiar sight in stores everywhere. Lauder continued her marketing efforts throughout the United States and Europe, and by 1970 her products were sold in seventy countries.

Lauder continued to run her hugely successful company well into the 1990s, assisted by her sons, who became involved in many charitable and Jewish causes. Her products are now sought out by millions of women. Her entire operation is based on the principle of personal care and of offering free samples, practices now common throughout the cosmetics industry. Like Rubinstein before her, Lauder has shown that having the right product, caring about the customer, and not being afraid to reach out and expand can make for great success in the business world.

Chapter Sixteen

Women in Sports

How many Jewish women have won Olympic medals or broken world records in sports? Not too many. The same is true of Jewish men. While some of the world's top athletes have been Jews of both genders, and while many Jews are great sports fans, cultivating sports champions has never seemed to be a Jewish tradition. The State of Israel, for example, has so far produced only one Olympic medalist, Yael Arad, who won the silver medal in women's judo at the Barcelona Olympics in 1992. But all of this may change in the future, as a growing number of young Jews throughout the world are getting more involved in sports than ever before.

Agnes Keleti

Here we will take a look at two Jewish women in the twentieth century who reached the top in the world of sports—Agnes Keleti and Irena Szewinska.

Women's gymnastics has become an extremely popular sport in the United States in recent years. Most female gymnasts peak in their teens and retire in their twenties. Due to circumstances, however, one of the greatest gymnasts of the century reached her peak between the ages of twenty-seven and thirty-five.

Her name is Agnes Keleti. She was born in Budapest, Hungary in 1921, the same year Hannah Szenes was born. While Szenes became a Zionist and immigrated to Palestine, where she would later become one of Israel's greatest heroes of the Holocaust, Keleti remained in Hungary where, at age fifteen, she joined a prestigious Jewish sports club and began to prepare for her career as a gymnast.

Keleti was determined to become a great athlete, but she knew she had many hurdles to overcome as a woman and as a Jew. In

1942 Hungary came under the Nazi sphere of influence, and all Jewish athletes were removed from the Hungarian national team. Keleti's career came to an abrupt end. In 1944 the Germans took control of Hungary and began deporting Hungarian Jews to concentration camps. Keleti's father and other relatives were taken away and died at Auschwitz. Keleti, her mother, and her sister were saved by Swedish diplomat Raoul Wallenberg, the most celebrated rescuer of Jews in World War II. They were given Christian documents and were able to leave Budapest, go into hiding, and survive the war.

After the war, Keleti, now twenty-six, returned to gymnastics. In 1946 she won her first Hungarian title in the uneven bars. Hungary was now a Communist country, and the Communists put great stock in sports. In the Cold War years, the Communist Bloc used sports as a channel of political propaganda, trying to gain the support of their people in what was a largely unpopular, oppressive regime, and show the "reactionary" capitalistic world that Communism was the right way. Consequently, promising athletes like Keleti received state support, enabling them to spend most of their time training. Because of her Keleti's ability, her Jewishness was overlooked. By 1947 she had become the leading gymnast in the Central European gymnastics championships.

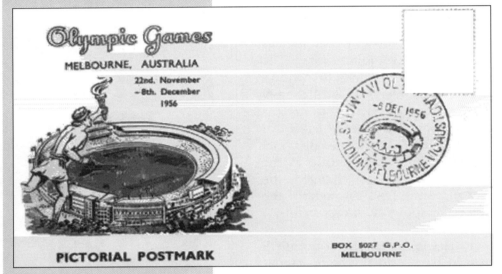

Postcard commemorating the 1956 Melbourne Olympics, where Keleti won five Olympic medals

In the 1948 London Olympics, Keleti won her first Olympic medals. In 1954 she became world champion of the uneven bars. By 1956 she had earned eleven medals, five of which were gold.

That same year, the Hungarians revolted against the Soviets and tried to overthrow Communism. The revolt was brutally suppressed by the Soviets. Keleti went to Australia at that time to participate in the Melbourne Olympics. There she won gold medals in the freestanding exercise, the balance beam exercise, the parallel bars, and the team combined exercise, as well as a silver medal in the combined exercise and team combined exercise (nine exercises). It was an incredible achievement for a woman of thirty-five.

Many Hungarian athletes decided not to return to Hungary and face life under the Soviets. Keleti was one of them. She defected and was given political asylum in Australia, where she stayed for about a year. In 1957 she went to Israel, where she settled and later brought her mother over and married a fellow Hungarian.

In Israel Keleti started a new athletic career. She organized the country's first teams of gymnasts and became a respected trainer. She continued to promote gymnastics in Israel well into the late 1990s. In 1991 she was invited back to Hungary to be inducted into the Hungarian Sports Hall of Fame. She is also a member of the Jewish Sports Hall of Fame in Israel.

❦   ❦   ❦

The Jewish Sports Hall of Fame also includes a Polish woman athlete named Irena Kirszenstein-Szewinska. Unlike Keleti, who had cast her lot with the Jewish people, Irena Szewinska, born in May 1945, after World War II and the Holocaust, had very little to do with the Jewish people. She happened to be born Jewish, and she grew up under the Communist regime in Poland, the same Communist regime that valued sports so highly for political reasons in Hungary, the Soviet Union, and other parts of the Communist Bloc. Szewinska received the best athletic training available and at age eighteen competed in the 1964 Tokyo Olympics, where she won silver medals in the 200-meter relay and the long jump, and a gold medal in the 400-meter relay. She would soon become the world's greatest track and field athlete.

Irena Szewinska

Over the next four years, Szewinska became a national hero in Poland. When she won important competitions and set world records, the Poles were quick to forget her Jewish background and took pride in her accomplishments.

In the 1968 Mexico City Olympics, Szewinska took the gold for the 200-meter race, setting a world record of 22.5 seconds. She also won the bronze in the 100-meter race.

123

She won more Olympic medals in the 1972 Munich Olympics and the 1976 Montreal Olympics, where she won the 400-meter race and set a world record of 49.29 seconds. This gave her her seventh Olympic medal. Szewinska won a total of seven Olympic medals, including three gold, as well as ten European medals (five gold), making her the most decorated woman athlete of all time.

Szewinska was back on the field in the 1980 Moscow Olympics, but she did not win more medals. She did, however, enter the annals of sport as one of the greatest women athletes, a totally dedicated person who reached the top in her field.

Chapter Seventeen

Women in Politics

At the close of the twentieth century, the United States, unlike Great Britain, India, and Israel, had never had a woman head of state. Women, however, had been active in local, state, and national politics in the U.S. for many years. Previously we saw how women like Lillian Wald and Emma Goldman were active in American politics early in the twentieth century. But it was not until the 1970s, when the women's rights movement started to make an impact on American life, that women began to find opportunities to attain high office. The last thirty years of the century saw the first woman on the Supreme Court, a growing number of congresswomen and female senators, and, as of 1971, the first Jewish woman member of the U.S. Congress. Her name was Bella Abzug.

When Bella Abzug died in 1998 at age seventy-seven, the *Associated Press* wrote:

> Former Rep. Bella Abzug, whose New York brass and wide-brimmed hats made her one of the most influential and recognizable leaders of the women's liberation movement in the 1970s, died Tuesday . . . "Bella was an original," said New York Mayor Edward I. Koch. "The women of the world, not just the country, owe her a great debt. She stood up for them as nobody else. She was their champion."

Bella Abzug was born Bella Savitzky in the Bronx in 1920. Her family was Orthodox, and the language spoken at home was Yiddish. As a teenager she joined the Zionist youth organization *Hashomer Hatzair* and dreamed of going to Israel and living on a kibbutz. Instead, she enrolled at Columbia Law

Bella Abzug

School and took evening Hebrew classes at the Jewish Theological Seminary. When the United States entered World War II, she dropped out of school and joined the war effort by working in a shipbuilding factory. Law school could wait, but defeating Hitler could not.

After the war, Abzug returned to her study of law at Columbia University, where she became editor of the school's *Law Review*. After passing the bar exam, Abzug decided to dedicate her life to social causes and help those in greatest need.

She specialized in labor and housing law and took on civil liberties cases. In one case, she tried to save the life of a black man sentenced to death in Mississippi for raping a white woman. In the early 1950s, blacks were excluded from juries in the South, and a fair trial for a black person was extremely hard to come by. Abzug challenged all of this, but she was ahead of her time and unable to stop the execution.

During the 1950s, when Senator Joseph McCarthy terrorized Washington with his witch hunt of imaginary Communists in government, Abzug defended several civil servants. A staunch Democrat and supporter of President Johnson, she became a strong activist against the Vietnam war in the 1960s, opposing Johnson's war policy. Her activism contributed to Johnson's decision not to seek reelection in 1968.

In 1970 Abzug was ready to run for national office. Being Jewish, a woman, highly controversial, and running against a seven-term incumbent, her chances were not very good. But the women's movement was gathering momentum, and Abzug ran on a feminist platform. Her election slogan was: "This woman belongs in the house—the House of Representatives." She won handily.

The 1970s were the Nixon years in America, not exactly Abzug's kind of a presidency. Later she wrote: "I was lonely and an oddity, a woman, a Jew, a New York lawyer, a feminist, a Nixon opponent from way back, a peace activist who passionately opposed American involvement in Indochina and just as strongly favored aid to democratic Israel."

But Abzug, an imposing presence with her wide-brimmed hats and her memorable statements, did make her mark on Congress and on America. At one point she said, "We don't so much want to see a female Einstein become an assistant professor. We want a woman *shlemiel* to get promoted as quickly as a male *shlemiel*." In her autobiography she wrote: "There are those who say I'm impatient, impetuous, uppity, rude, profane, brash, and overbearing. Whether I'm any of these things or all of them, you can decide for yourself. But whatever I am, and this ought to be made very clear at the outset, I am a very serious woman."

When the United Nations passed its infamous resolution calling Zionism "racism," Abzug denounced it publicly. She said, "Judaism has had a very profound affect on me. Jews believe you can't have justice for yourself unless other people have justice as well. That has motivated much of what I've done."

In 1976 Abzug lost a senatorial primary. She continued to practice law, and worked for many liberal causes in the U.S. and around the world. To the end, she was an impassioned champion of women's rights. She believed deeply that in the twenty-first century women would play a leading role in every sphere of human endeavor.

☙ ☙ ☙

If anyone had said thirty years ago that someday the state of California would be represented in the U.S. Senate by two women, he or she would have been dismissed as a cockeyed feminist. If that person had gone a step further and said that both women would be Jewish, no one would have listened. The odds against it, after all, were huge. But this is exactly what happened in 1992, when Barbara Boxer joined Dianne Feinstein in the U.S. Senate, marking the first time any state had sent two women to the upper house, let alone two Jewish women.

By the time Dianne Feinstein arrived in Washington, she was already a national figure in American politics. Born in San Francisco in 1933 to a Jewish father and a Russian Orthodox mother, she was educated in a Catholic school. But she chose her father's religion and might therefore be considered "a Jew by choice."

While in college, Feinstein decided to dedicate her life to public service. She specialized in criminal justice, and from 1962 to 1966 she served as vice chairperson of the California Women's Board of Terms and Parole. She became active in city politics in her native San Francisco, and in 1971, at age thirty-eight, she ran for mayor and finished third. She tried again four years later but lost.

[I would like to be remembered] as a mayor who did her best to make San Francisco a better place to live . . . and created an effective role model for women in executive positions.
—Dianne Feinstein

Courtesy of The Washington Jewish Week

Senator Dianne Feinstein with Israeli Prime Minister Shimon Peres

127

In 1978, when Mayor George Moscone was assassinated by a city employee, Feinstein became acting mayor and drew national attention. She was selected by the city's Board of Supervisors to complete Moscone's term, thereby becoming the first woman mayor in the city's history. The following year she won the mayoral race and soon became known as one of the most liberal mayors in the country.

In 1990 Feinstein ran for governor of California. She campaigned long and hard, but lost. Determined not to let her political career die, in 1992 she ran for the United States Senate. She played up her being a woman and a Jew, insisting that having only two women in a one-hundred-member Senate is not enough. She defeated the Republican candidate, John Seymour, by a very wide margin.

During her years in the Senate, Feinstein promoted public safety, and authored the Gun Free Schools Act and the Hate Crimes Sentencing Enhancement Act, the first designed to rid schools of guns, and the second to increase penalties for hate crimes. Feinstein clearly succeeded in proving what she had set out to prove, namely, that a Jewish woman can be a force for good in the U.S. Senate.

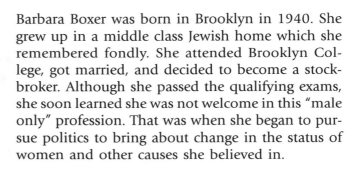

Barbara Boxer was born in Brooklyn in 1940. She grew up in a middle class Jewish home which she remembered fondly. She attended Brooklyn College, got married, and decided to become a stockbroker. Although she passed the qualifying exams, she soon learned she was not welcome in this "male only" profession. That was when she began to pursue politics to bring about change in the status of women and other causes she believed in.

Senator Barbara Boxer (right) with Senator Dianne Feinstein

On a visit to California, Boxer felt she had found the right state where a woman could be successful in effecting change. She persuaded her husband to move with her to California, where he pursued his legal career. She soon became involved in civic causes, worked at the weekly newspaper *Pacific Sun,* and served as a district aide to Representative John Burton, a Democrat.

In 1976 Boxer began her perfect record of winning elected office when she became the first woman president of the Marin County Board of Supervisors. In 1982 she won a

128

seat in Congress and went on to serve for five terms. She first made a name for herself in Congress when she discovered that the Pentagon had spent $7,600 on the purchase of a coffeepot. She went on to fight against overspending on tanks and bombers, which until then had gone largely unquestioned in the male-dominated House.

In 1992 Boxer ran for Senate on the platform of women's rights. She advocated abortion rights, environmental protection, and cuts in military spending. It was a tough race, but she won by a narrow margin and joined Dianne Feinstein in representing California in the Senate.

In 1998 Boxer won reelection by a large margin. She had become known for promoting California's economy. She took a strong stand on education, seeking to ensure that every child can read by age eight, use a computer by age twelve, and attend college by age eighteen. She authored the Patient's Bill of Rights and the Freedom of Choice Act for women.

Boxer was recognized as an "Outstanding Mother" by the National Mothers' Day Committee, and was hailed as a champion of human rights by the Anti-Defamation League, the Human Rights Campaign Fund, and the Leadership Conference on Civil Rights.

Women like Barbara Boxer and Dianne Feinstein have certainly fulfilled the vision of Bella Abzug, who predicted that in the twenty-first century women would be taking the lead in areas previously dominated by men.

Congratulations on the signing of the Wye River Memorandum ... which is also, hopefully, a beginning of a new era of peace in the Middle East.
—Barbara Boxer, in a letter to President Bill Clinton (October 23, 1998)

Tuoro Synagogue, Newport, Rhode Island—the oldest synagogue in the United States (dedicated in 1763)—displays a letter from George Washington welcoming people of the Jewish faith to their new homeland.

Chapter Eighteen

Women in Law

One area where women have made great progress in our time is law. In 1976, the first woman was appointed to the Supreme Court in Israel. A few years later, the first woman was appointed to the Supreme Court in the United States. Then, in 1993, a Jewish woman became the second woman ever appointed to that court. Clearly, when given the opportunity, women can compete with the best legal minds and attain the highest positions in the legal system.

Miriam Ben-Porat, the first woman ever to serve on Israel's Supreme Court, received the Israel Prize in 1991 for her special contribution to society and state. Born in Russia in 1918, Ben-Porat immigrated to Palestine in 1936. She studied law under the British Mandatory system and earned her law degree in 1945. In 1948, the same year Israel was established, she was employed by the State Attorney's office and served there until 1953, when she became Deputy State Attorney. In 1958 she was appointed judge of the district court in Jerusalem. From 1964 to 1978 she taught law at Hebrew University.

Ben-Porat was appointed to the Israeli Supreme Court in 1976 and served for seven years before becoming deputy president of the court. In Israel, the Supreme Court is a highly respected body of jurists who safeguard the rule of law in the Jewish state. Israel is a young democracy which seeks to accommodate a wide range of Jews, from the most religious to the most secular, from those most accustomed to living in a democracy to those who have never lived under a democratic system. It also has a large Arab population consisting of both Israeli citizens and Palestinians living under Israeli occupation. In addition, Israel has a variety of Christian and other religious minorities, such as Druze. Quite often, the Israeli

Miriam Ben-Porat

Supreme Court has had to take strong stands on highly sensitive cases, often in direct opposition to policies of the Israeli government. During her years on the court, Ben-Porat became an expert in dealing with such cases and maintaining the delicate balance of Israeli society.

This expertise resulted in her election by the Knesset in 1988 to the highly sensitive position of State Comptroller and Public Complaints Commissioner. The task of the state comptroller is to ensure that government agencies are doing their job properly. The Knesset probably did not expect Ben-Porat to revolutionize her new position. While her predecessors had taken a lukewarm attitude and avoided confrontations, Ben-Porat did not hesitate to focus attention on even the highest government officials. She exposed waste, inefficiency, and at times even criminal behavior, and quickly became the state official "most politicians love to hate."

Among other issues, she was very vocal on women's rights and on the issue of absorbing new Russian immigrants. She did not spare either the Israeli right or the left, and made enemies of both. But this did not seem to bother her. She had a job to do, and she was going to do it to the best of her ability, without kowtowing to anyone.

Begrudgingly, many eventually recognized Ben-Porat's integrity and her contribution to bettering the Israeli government system. When she received the Israel Prize in 1991 for her special contribution to society and state, she was given a standing ovation. Her unpopular work was fully appreciated, and in 1993 she was elected for another five-year term as state comptroller.

Ben-Porat's record as Israel's state comptroller stands out in Israeli society as a great accomplishment, one worthy of emulating by both men and women.

❦ ❦ ❦

Historically, the United States Supreme Court, which consists of nine members, has had one Jewish justice, always a male. Some, like Louis Brandeis, Benjamin Cardozo, and Felix Frankfurter, were among the court's outstanding legal minds. It was only recently, in 1993, that a Jewish woman was appointed to the court. Her name is Ruth Bader Ginsburg.

Ruth was born in Brooklyn in 1933. As a child she was an avid reader and deeply aware of the tragedy visited upon her

I am responsible to the people, not to those who defame me.
—Miriam Ben-Porat

132

people in Europe. She became sensitized to the need for justice in a world where people can easily lose their civil rights.

An outstanding student, she attended Cornell University, and in 1956 enrolled in Harvard Law School. At Harvard she became aware for the first time of discrimination against women in the legal profession. She transferred from Harvard to Columbia Law School when her husband, an attorney, obtained a job with a law firm in New York. In 1959 she graduated first in her class from Columbia Law School, only to find that not a single law firm in New York was interested in employing her. Subsequently, she became a clerk to a judge of the U.S. District Court.

In 1960, the dean of Harvard Law School proposed that Ginsburg, whom he held in high esteem, be hired as law clerk to Supreme Court Justice Felix Frankfurter. Unfortunately, Frankfurter was not prepared to hire a woman and declined.

Ginsburg then turned to teaching law at Rutgers Law School. Paid less than her male colleagues, she joined female faculty members in a legal case that resulted in higher salaries for women teachers.

In 1972 Ginsburg founded the Women's Rights Project of the American Civil Liberties Union. Her objective was to show that the law discriminates between men and women even when it is unconstitutional to do so. Before the U.S. Supreme Court later that year, she challenged the discharge of a pregnant officer in the Air Force. Ginsburg won several women's rights cases before that court, greatly helping further the cause of equality for women in American society.

In 1992, President Bill Clinton appointed Ruth Bader Ginsburg to the Supreme Court. She joined Sandra Day O'Connor as the second female justice. Ginsburg aptly observed that having two women on the court made it seem natural to have both genders, rather than an oddity. Equality between men and women in the legal field was finally becoming a reality.

A lawyer can do something that is personally satisfying and at the same time work to preserve the values that make this country great.
—Ruth Bader Ginsburg

Courtesy of *The Washington Jewish Week*

Justice Ruth Bader Ginsburg receives an award from Hadassah.

133

Hebrew Union College in Cincinnati, Ohio (Reform), was the first major rabbinical seminary in the world to ordain women (1972).

The Jewish Theological Seminary in New York City (Conservative) followed suit a few years later.

Chapter Nineteen

Women Rabbis

In 1972 the Hebrew Union College in Cincinnati, Ohio ordained the first woman rabbi. It was the first time this title was officially conferred on a woman. Before long, other rabbinical schools in America, such as the Conservative Jewish Theological Seminary, began to ordain women. Over the next twenty-five years, the number of women rabbis in America grew, and today nearly half of the rabbinical students in non-Orthodox schools are women. The impact of women rabbis on American Jewish religious life has been profound. It is quite possible that in the twenty-first century women will revitalize Jewish religious practices and deepen Jewish spirituality.

The women's revolution did not skip Orthodox women in the U.S., in Israel, and around the world. A growing number of Orthodox women have been pursuing religious studies and seeking a more active role in Jewish religious life. There is no law in Judaism preventing a woman from assuming a role of religious leadership, and it is quite possible that even among Orthodox Jews women may begin to play a more active role in years to come.

The following is the personal testimony of Rabbi Tobie Weisman, a member of the new generation of women rabbis in the United States. Rabbi Weisman lives in Vermont.

❦ ❦ ❦

Torah case, France (1860); scroll, Spain (seventeenth century)

Courtesy of the Jewish Museum, New York

135

Sabbath candlesticks (bronze)
by Ludwig Y. Wolpert

I never dreamed of becoming a rabbi. It was just not a possibility for me since I was born a girl and raised as a traditional Jew. While I remember hating the fact that because I was a girl, I could not have an *aliyah* to the Torah for my bat mitzvah, I did not let myself even imagine that in my lifetime, there would be such phenomenal changes for Jewish women.

If I had seen women as rabbis and cantors, I'm sure I would have thought of following that path. Looking back on my childhood and upbringing, it was the natural progression of my life.

I was blessed with a spiritually rich Jewish home. I was very close with my grandmother. Without knowing it, she was a radical Jewish feminist. She graduated in the first class of professional Jewish women Hebrew teachers in America. A woman studying Torah at that time was practically unheard of. She was always writing me letters in Hebrew (with translations) and telling me Jewish stories. My father, in addition to his Jewish communal work, has always taken great pleasure in serving as *hazzan*, or cantor. I have an early memory of my father *davening* on the High Holidays. Watching him *daven*, I remember being awed by the thought that he was really praying to God. I wanted to be able to pray to God, too. My mother included me in her vision of helping the elderly Jewish residents of a nursing home create lives of meaning for themselves. She introduced me to a number of residents with whom I developed and maintained close relationships, even throughout and after college.

In college, all that interested me was Jewish studies. I ended up majoring in Hebrew and Jewish studies, with no idea of how I would use it as a career. I simply loved the learning. I did have a flash of thought when one of my friends in college announced that she would be going to rabbinical school. I remember thinking, "I cannot do that because am not a Reform Jew." I didn't give it any further thought.

After college I began working as a computer programmer. I had no idea what I should do as a career, but I knew that a career in computers was not for me. I became very involved in a *havurah* called Fabrengen in Washington, D.C. There I learned how to lead services, read Torah, and teach. I loved becoming a leader in the community and was encouraged by my friends to pursue becoming a rabbi. My parents were extremely opposed to it and did not support this wild idea of mine. There was finally such a strong push within me that it was impossible to ignore it any longer. I decided to learn traditional Jewish texts at a place called Pardes in Israel. There I learned how to listen to God's voice through the words of the texts I was studying. I began to develop my own response to Jewish observance based on my experience of these texts and by watching how the texts lived in the teachers who taught them. I began to have a relationship with God that was both difficult and uncomfortable as well as tangible and grounded.

After returning from Pardes, it took me six more years to finally go to rabbinical school. Even though doors were opened to women in the Conservative movement, there was still a lot of animosity towards women in the rabbinate. I kept telling myself that I could do other things. Finally, while I was working as a program director for rabbinical and cantorial students at the Jewish Theological Seminary, I realized these students were doing what the still small voice inside me was crying out to do. I had to go to rabbinical school, even if I would never practice as a rabbi.

While in rabbinical school, I met Rabbi Shlomo Carlebach on the street one day. I had become very involved in his *shul* and felt inspired by his teachings from the Hasidic *rebbes*. He asked me how I was doing. I excitedly shared with him that I was going to rabbinical school. He smiled and looked at me lovingly and asked, "Are they teaching you what brings life?"

That question remained with me as my mantra throughout rabbinical school and until this day. The teachings that "brought life" came mainly from the experiences I had as a rabbinical intern in a nursing home and a hospital, and later as a student rabbi. I learned that having the title "rabbi" gave me a way to be invited into people's spiritual lives like no other title would. I was able to be with people during such precious times as life cycle passages, illness and healing, weddings, births, and deaths. Sometimes just sitting with people and listening to them speak about their lives could be full of holiness, awe, and wonder. At these times, I often would feel the presence of God stronger than ever.

Being a woman rabbi has helped people feel more open with me than if I had been a man. Many women have told me that they would not have felt comfortable speaking to a male rabbi about certain issues. Even some men have told me this. Young women and girls seeing me as a rabbi realize the opportunities their own future holds.

There have been and still are difficulties being a woman rabbi. Many people still believe a rabbi should be a man with

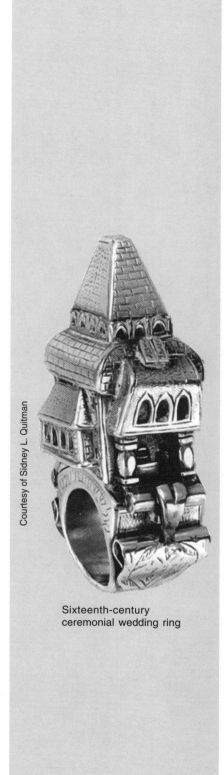

Courtesy of Sidney L. Quitman

Sixteenth-century
ceremonial wedding ring

a beard and a low booming voice. This image will take a long time to change.

I have worked as a congregational rabbi in New York, Maryland, and Vermont. I now have a freelance rabbinical practice where I am hired to teach, speak, lead services and life cycle ceremonies, and counsel people on spiritual issues. The counseling experiences that I had as an intern led me to pursue a degree in counseling. So now I am also a family and child therapist at a nearby public school.

I have no doubt that I did the right thing. Almost every day, someone asks me a question or tells me their story or needs to talk about something that connects them to Jewish life or to their spirituality. For many people, I might be the person that allows them to come back to their Jewish roots or to help them gain a deeper understanding of Judaism.

Becoming a rabbi has given me the tools with which to learn the deepest teachings from our tradition and share those teachings with others. But the real teachings have come from life itself. I have just experienced one of life's deepest teachings: the miracle of giving birth to a baby daughter. Who knows? Maybe all my training and all my experiences in my journey of becoming a rabbi have led me to this moment.

As it says in the *shema* prayer, "*V'shinantam l'vanecha,*" "And you shall teach them [words of Torah] to your children." How do we teach Torah to our children? By setting an example of being the best possible Jew we can be. And how do we know how to be the best Jew we can be? By seeing every experience of our lives as a new revelation from God on Mount Sinai.

My spiritual story does not end with my becoming a rabbi. This was a fundamental part of my travels, but not the final destination. I am so grateful that the doors of Jewish tradition opened for me when I needed to enter them to continue my journey.

Chapter *Twenty*

Jewish Women in the Twenty-first Century

We have traveled a long way, from the days of Sarah and Abraham to the end of the twentieth century. The history of our people has seen many twists and turns, many ups and downs, many high hopes dashed against the rocks of reality. But ours has always been an optimistic faith. In the twentieth century our people experienced the greatest disaster ever, the destruction of the Jews in Europe, commonly known as the Holocaust. But we have also been blessed with what may well have been the greatest event of the past two millennia, the birth of the State of Israel. Finally having a state of their own, our people were able to rescue millions of Jews from war-ravaged Europe, from the Arab world, and, more recently, from the countries of the former Soviet Union and from Ethiopia. And at century's end there is hope that Arabs and Jews may at long last live side by side in peace.

We Jews have always been aware not only of our own welfare, but also of the welfare of others. Our prophets taught us that all people are children of God. Only when all people are free are we too free. And, indeed, there are far more free nations in the world today than there were only fifty years ago, or even ten years ago.

One of the great successful revolutions of the twentieth century has been the women's revolution. Early in the century, women fought for the right to vote, to be recognized as men's equals. But it was not until the 1970s that the women's rights movement truly came into its own in the United States. As before in history at times of great social change, Jewish women were again in the forefront. Feminism became a force which altered society, and started the process of creating equality for women in the workplace, in politics, in every area of human activity.

The impact of feminism has been felt in the many ethnic, religious, social, and cultural communities in the United States and in other countries, and has had a profound effect on Jewish life.

Today's young Jewish women will come of age in a world entirely different from that of their mothers, as women continue to narrow the gap between themselves and the male world. While women have always played a vital role in the Jewish community, in

the twenty-first century their role will become even more vital. The opportunities for Jewish women in both the general and the Jewish community will be unlimited. No longer restricted by a male dominated world, they will be able to freely apply all their talents and realize their full potential. They may not only achieve parity with men, but in many areas even surpass them. And there is little doubt that the Jewish community will be greatly enriched as a result, and so will the rest of the world.

Having said this, let us keep in mind that there is still much work to be done to make all these things a reality. Many Jewish women are still not free or equal, and entire nations still suffer from poverty, hunger, and oppression. In the new century, we will need more great Jewish women to follow the path of their predecessors in past centuries, for their own people and for the entire world. Some readers of this book may well be those women. Hopefully, more than a few young women who have read these pages will be inspired to apply their talents and their energy toward *tikkun olam,* or perfecting the world in the image of God. This has always been the mission of Judaism. Blessed is the daughter who will make it her mission in the years to come.

$\mathcal{A}$ppendix

Jewish Women's Organizations and Jewish Youth Organizations

Agudah Women of America
84 William Street, New York, NY 10038

Organizes Jewish women for philanthropic work in the U.S. and Israel and for intensive Torah education. The Girls' Division (Bnos Agudath) sponsors regular weekly programs on the local level and unites girls from throughout the Torah world with extensive regional and national activities.

B'nai B'rith Youth Organization
1640 Rhode Island Avenue NW, Washington, DC 20036

Helps Jewish teenagers achieve self-fulfillment and make a maximum contribution to the Jewish community and their country's culture. Helps members acquire a greater knowledge and appreciation of Jewish religion and culture. Maintains a summer camp program in New York and Wisconsin, conducts leadership programs for youth and Israel travel summer program. The girls' division of BBYO is B'nai B'rith Girls, or BBG.

Emuna of America
7 Penn Plaza, New York, NY 10001

Formerly Hapoel Hamizrachi Women's Organization. This organization of Orthodox women maintains and supports two hundred educational and social welfare institutions in Israel within a religious framework, including day care centers, kindergartens, children's residential homes, vocational schools for the underprivileged, senior-citizen centers, a college complex, and a Holocaust study center. Also involved in the absorption of Soviet and Ethiopian immigrants.

Hadassah
50 West 58th Street, New York, NY 10019

Hadassah, The Women's Zionist Organization of America, is the largest Jewish women's organization in the United States. It maintains the Hadassah Medical Organization in Jerusalem and the Hadassah College of Technology. It operates the Hadassah Career Counseling Institute and runs the summer and year-long Young Judea programs. U.S. programs include Jewish and health education, leadership training, advocacy for Israel, Zionist and women's studies, and six Young Judea summer camps. Young Judea is a religious pluralist youth organization. It seeks to educate Jewish youth ages 8-25 toward Jewish and Zionist values, active commitment and participation in the American and Israeli Jewish communities. It runs both summer and year-long programs in Israel in cooperation with Hebrew University in Jerusalem and Ben-Gurion University of the Negev. A college-age arm, Hamagshimim, supports Zionist activity on campuses.

Hashomer Hatzair

114 West 26th Street, Suite 1001, New York, NY 10001

Dedicated to educating Jewish youth in the understanding of Zionism as the national liberation movement of the Jewish people. Promotes *aliyah* to kibbutzim. Affiliated with the American Zionist Youth Federation (AZYF) and the Kibbutz Artzi Federation. Pursues socialist-Zionist ideals of peace, justice, democracy, and intergroup harmony.

Hillel: The Foundation for Jewish Campus Life

1640 Rhode Island Avenue NW, Washington, DC 20036

The largest Jewish campus organization in the world, with a network of five hundred regional centers, campus-based foundations, and affiliates which serve Jewish college students in promoting Jewish living, culture, and religion.

Jewish Women International (formerly *B'nai B'rith Women*)

1828 L Street NW, Suite 250, Washington, DC 20036

Strengthens the lives of women, children, and families through education, advocacy, and action. Focuses on family violence and the emotional health of children. JWI serves as an agent for change—locally, nationally, and around the world. Offers programs in the U.S., Canada, and Israel.

Na'amat USA

200 Madison Avenue, 21st Floor, New York, NY 10016

Part of Na'amat (worldwide movement of working women and volunteers), the largest Jewish women's organization in the world. Na'amat USA helps provide social, educational, and legal services for women, teenagers, and children in Israel. It also advocates legislation for women's rights and child welfare in Israel and the U.S., furthers Jewish education, and supports Habonim Dror, the Labor Zionist youth movement.

National Conference of Synagogue Youth

333 Seventh Avenue, New York, NY 10001

Central body for youth groups of Orthodox congregations. Provides educational guidance, Torah study groups, community service, libraries, scholarships, week-long seminars, Israel summer stays for teens, and camp programs.

National Jewish Girl Scout Committee

33 Central Drive, Bronxville, NY 10708

Serves to further Jewish education by developing Jewish award programs, encouraging religious services, promoting cultural exchanges with the Israel Boy and Girl Scout Federation, and extending membership in the Jewish community by assisting councils in organizing Girl Scout troops and local Jewish Girl Scout Committees.

Pioneer Women/Na'amat. See Na'amat USA.

Re'uth Women's Social Service

130 East 59th Street, New York, NY 10022

Maintains subsidized housing for self-reliant elderly in Israel, homes for dependent elderly, the Lichtenstadter Hospital for chronically ill and young accident victims not accepted by other hospitals, organizes subsidized meals and Golden Age clubs.

United Synagogue Youth

155 Fifth Avenue, New York, NY 10010

Dedicated to strengthening youth identification with Conservative Judaism, based on the personality development, needs, and interests of adolescents, in a *mitzvah* framework. Consisting of more than five hundred chapters, it sponsors regional conferences, ten summer camps, a national convention, and an Israel Pilgrimage.

US-Israel Women to Women

275 Seventh Avenue, 8th Floor, New York, NY 10001

Provides financial support for grassroots advocacy of equal status and fair treatment for women in all spheres of Israeli life. Targets small, innovative, Israeli-run programs that seek to bring about social change in health, education, civil rights, domestic violence, family planning, and other spheres of Israeli life.

Women of Reform Judaism - The Federation of Temple Sisterhoods

633 Third Avenue, New York, NY 10017

Serves more than six hundred sisterhoods of Reform congregations. Promotes interreligious understanding and social justice, provides scholarship funding for rabbinical students, provides braille and large-type Judaic materials for Jewish blind, supports projects in Israel.

Women's American ORT

315 Park Avenue South, New York, NY 10010

ORT is the world's largest nongovernmental education and training organization. It has a global network of over 262,000 students in more than sixty countries. In Israel, 100,000 students attend 138 schools and training centers. There are twenty-two ORT schools in the former Soviet Union. In the U.S., over 10,000 students are served by ORT's Technical Institutes in Chicago, Los Angeles, and New York.
The women's arm of ORT is engaged in membership drives, fundraising, and educational activities. Its domestic agenda includes quality public education, women's rights, and the national literacy campaign.

Women's Branch of the Union of Orthodox Jewish Congregations

156 Fifth Avenue, New York, NY 10010

Umbrella organization of Orthodox sisterhoods in the U.S. and Canada, educating women in Jewish learning and observance, providing programing, leadership, and organizational guidance. Supports Stern and Touro College scholarships and Jewish braille publications.

Women's Division of Poale Agudath Israel of America

2920 Avenue J, Brooklyn, NY 11210

Assists Poale Agudath Israel in building and supporting children's homes, kindergartens, and trade schools in Israel.

Women's League for Conservative Judaism

48 East 74th Street, New York, NY 10021

Parent body of Conservative women's synagogue groups in the U.S., Canada, Mexico, and Israel. Provides programs and resources in Jewish education, social action, Israel affairs, American and Canadian public affairs, leadership training, community service, and study institutes. Supports the Jewish Theological Seminary.

Women's League for Israel

160 East 56th Street, New York, NY 10022

Maintains centers in Haifa, Tel Aviv, Jerusalem, and Natanya. Projects include Family Therapy and Training Center, Centers for the Prevention of Domestic Violence, and Meeting Places (supervised centers for non-custodial parents and their children). Supports families at risk, long-term therapy for parents and children, Central Training School for Training Social Service Couselors, the National Library for Social Work, and the Hebrew University Blind Students' Unit.

Young Israel Department of Youth and Young Adults Activities

3 West 16th Street, New York, NY 10011

Promotes a variety of activities for the perpetuation of Torah-true Judaism. Instills ethical and spiritual values and an appreciation for the compatibility of American life and the ancient faith of Israel. Runs leadership training programs and youth *shabbatonim*, summer programs for teens, Nachala summer program in Israel for yeshiva high school girls, and Natzach summer program for yeshiva high school boys.

Young Judea. See *Hadassah*.

Youth Division and North American Federation of Temple Youth

633 Third Avenue, New York, NY 10017

Dedicated to providing Jewish programs for the youth of Reform congregations through informal education conducted in youth camp-institutes throughout the United States (ten camps), and NFTY summer and semester programs in Israel.

Bibliography

Ashton, Dianne. *Rebecca Gratz: Women and Judaism in Antebellum America.* Michigan: Waye State University, 1997.

Babylonian Talmud, The. English translation edited by Rabbi Dr. I. Epstein. London: Soncino Press, 1948-52.

Bacall, Lauren. *Lauren Bacall: By Myself.* New York: Ballantine Books, 1994.

Bernhardt, Sarah, and Victoria Tietze Larson. *My Double Life: The Memoirs of Sarah Bernhardt.* New York: State University of New York, 1999.

Chalberg, John C. *Emma Goldman: American Individualist.* New York: HarperCollins, 1995.

Chicago, Judy. *Holocaust Project: From Darkness into Light.* New York: Penguin, 1993.

Cohen, Geulah. *Sipurah shel lohemet (Fighter's Story).* Tel Aviv: Karni, 1975.

Coss, Clare. *Lillian D. Wald: Progressive Activist.* New York: Feminine Press, 1989.

Cowen, Ida, and Irena Gunther. *The Story of Sarah Aaronsohn.* N.p., n.d.

Darmouth Bible, The. Boston: Houghton Mifflin, 1961.

Eliot, George. *Daniel Deronda.* New York: Penguin, 1997.

Frank, Anne. *Diary of a Young Girl.* New York: Bantam, 1997.

Gratz, Rebecca. *Letters of Rebecca Gratz.* North Stratford, New Hampshire: Ayer Co., 1975.

Hameln, Glueckel of. *Memoirs of Glueckel of Hameln.* New York: Schocken, 1988.

Head, Dominic. *Nadine Gordimer.* Cambridge: Cambridge University Press, 1995.

Henry, Christopher E. *Ruth Bader Ginsburg.* Danbury, Connecticut: Franklin Watts, 1994.

Hess, Thomas B., and Elizabeth C. Baker, eds. *Art and Sexual Politics: Why Have There Been No Great Women Artists?* New York: Collier, 1973.

Hyman, Paula, and Deborah Dash Moore, eds. *Jewish Women in America: An Historical Encyclopedia.* New York: Routledge, 1997.

Krantz, Hazel. *Daughter of My People: Henrietta Szold and Hadassah.* Northvale, New Jersey: Jason Aronson, 1998.

Leibowitz, Nehama. *Studies in Genesis.* Jerusalem: World Zionist Organization, 1981.

Lubetkin, Zivia. *In the Days of Destruction and Revolt.* Tel Aviv: Ghetto Fighters' House, 1981.

Meir, Golda. *My Life.* New York: G. P. Putnam's Sons, 1975.

Minkin, Jacob S. *The Romance of Hassidism.* New York: Thomas Yoseloff, 1955.

Perl, Lila. *Molly Picon: A Gift of Laughter.* Philadelphia: Jewish Publication Society, 1990.

Plaskow, Judith. *Standing Again at Sinai.* San Francisco: HarperSanFrancisco, 1991.

Ra'hel. *Shirat Ra'hel (Ra'hel's Poetry).* Tel Aviv: Davar, 1950.

Ravikovitch, Dahlia. *Kol hashirim ad ko (Complete Poems So Far).* Tel Aviv: Hakibbutz Hameuchad, 1996.

Riese, Randall. *Her Name Is Barbra: Portrait of the Real Barbra Streisand.* New York: Birch Lane, 1993.

Roth, Cecil. *Doña Gracia: The House of Nasi.* Philadelphia: Jewish Publication Society, 1992.

Sachs, Nelly. *O the Chimneys.* New York: Farrar, Straus and Giroux, 1967.

Slater, Robert. *Great Jews in Sports.* New York: Jonathan David, 1991.

———. *Great Jewish Women.* New York: Jonathan David, 1998.

Syrkin, Marie. *Blessed is the Match: The Story of Jewish Resistance.* Philadelphia: Jewish Publication Society, 1976.

Taitz, Emily, and Sondra Henry. *Remarkable Jewish Women: Rebels, Rabbis, and Other Women from Biblical Times to the Present.* Philadelphia: Jewish Publication Society, 1996.

TaNaKh (Hebrew Bible). Jerusalem: Koren, 1996.

Young, Bette Roth. *Emma Lazarus in the New World: Life and Letters.* Philadelphia: Jewish Publication Society, 1997.

Index